LDS Puzzle Pals

LDS Puzzle Pals

MaryAlice Wallis and
C. G. Lindstrom

CFI

Springville, Utah

This puzzle book is lovingly dedicated to our children:
Tyler, Adam, Amanda, Elizabeth, Steven, and Alex.

ISBN 13: 978-1-55517-994-6

Published by CFI, an imprint of Cedar Fort, Inc., 2373 W. 700 S., Springville, UT, 84663
Distributed by Cedar Fort, Inc., www.cedarfort.com

Cover design by Nicole Williams
Edited and typeset by Kimiko M. Hammari
Cover design © 2007 by Lyle Mortimer

Printed in the United States of America

10 9 8 7 6 5 4 3 2 1

Printed on acid-free paper

Table of Contents

CALLED OF GOD TO BAPTIZE

Hidden Message

For this is he that was spoken of by
the prophet Esias.
—Matthew 3:3

Circle every other letter on the top line, beginning with the first letter, to reveal an important person in the scriptures.

J R O K H S N U T S H L E C B L A I P D T X I E S E T

__ __ __ __   __ __ __   __ __ __ __ __ __ __

Circle every third letter on the bottom line, beginning with the third letter, to reveal a place important to this famous person.

P L R N E I J E V U Z E J C R Y W J M I O W B R Z G D Q E A P E N

__ __ __ __ __   __ __ __ __ __ __

Clean and Pure

Word Search

Except a man be born of water and
of the Spirit, he cannot enter into the
kingdom of God.

—John 3:5

C H U R C H O F J E S U S C H R I S T E

R I S W J K I D R E P E N T A N C E B A

G N M D K N R W Q P U R O L T J M L X C

L T K M I S S I O N A R I E S L Y D G O

D E O R E F H N R E Q X S H O F P T Y M

W R Q U K R R E Q B M B A P T I Z E D M

U V L P I L S E D I U D C W L G W M S A

W I A R F D C I N A O W R P T I C E P N

O E H A V W R G O O S B A U F K S J S D

R W P Y U P Z H H N K G M Y R S D I R M

T D L E V U E T Y P M V E A E R B T W E

H H E R N I S O E L E R N N I T U V T N

Y B N T R E C H O O S E T H E R I G H T

A D X O I W D F R E C I J F L C K V A S

B S N R A E S P H I W A T E R F S E M U

T Z P U R I T Y D Z L P M R H O A Y B L

R X L A Z C N H S K R L I W U G L I J I

J O H N T H E B A P T I S T U S U P T M

E T S M B I W W Y U B L T K D E L Q U H

A G I F T O F T H E H O L Y G H O S T W

Baptized
Choose the Right
Church of Jesus Christ
Commandments
Eight
Faith
Gift of the Holy Ghost
Immersion
Interview
John the Baptist
Missionaries
Prayer
Priesthood
Purity
Repentance
Sacrament
Water
Witnesses
Worthy

Elements of Baptism

Missing Letter Words

The disciples whom Jesus had chosen began from
that time forth to baptize and to teach as many as
did come unto them; and as many as were baptized in
the name of Jesus were filled with the Holy Ghost.
—3 Nephi 26:17

Every other letter is missing from the words below. The letters are listed in alphabetical order in the box beside the phrase. Replace each blank to find phrases that tell about how and why we are baptized. The scripture references have the answers if you get stuck.

1. a __r__k__n __e__r__ a__d __ c__n__r__t__ s__i__i__ (Moroni 6:2)

a a b e e h i n o o p r t t t

2. b__p__i__e__ e__e__ b__ w__t__r (D&C 33:11)

a a d e n t v y z

3. __a__t__s__ o__ f__r__ a__d __h__ H__l__ G__o__t (D&C 39:6)

b e e f h i i m n o p s t y

4. a__t__o__i__y __r__m Jesus Christ __o __a__t__z__ (D&C 20:73)

b e f h i o p r t t u

5. p__e__c__ r__p__n__a__c__ a__d __e__i__s__o__ o__ s__n__ (D&C 55:2)

a e e e f h i i m n n n r r s s t

FIRST THINGS FIRST

Matching

• • • • • • • • • • • • • • • • •

Match the following words on the left with the phrase and scripture reference on the right. Put the word that corresponds with each numbered answer in the blanks to fill in the scripture at the end of the puzzle.

Faith	2. Jesus came to Galilee to preach this (Mark 1:14).
Gospel	1. Moses was commanded to teach these (Exodus 18:20).
Ordinances	6. This shall teach you all things (John 14:26).
Immersion	4. Confessing and forsaking sins (D&C 58:43).
Holy Ghost	5. Process of going down into the water completely (3 Nephi 11:16–30).
Repentance	3. Things hoped for but not seen (Hebrews 11:1).

The first principles and ________________ (1) of the ________________ (2) are: first, ______________ (3) in the Lord Jesus Christ; second ________________ (4); third, Baptism by ________________ (5) for the remission of sins; fourth, Laying on of hands for the gift of the ________________ (6) (Articles of Faith 1:4).

Follow Jesus Christ

Letter Clue

Come unto me, and believe in my
gospel, and be baptized in my name.
—Ether 4:18

Write the word for each definition. Then write the numbered letters below to complete a scripture about baptism. Look it up when you're through!

1. The Savior of mankind ___ ___ ___ ___ ___   ___ ___ ___ ___ ___ ___ (numbered blanks: 15, 6, 21, 37, 30)

2. Asking for forgiveness; changing ___ ___ ___ ___ ___ ___ ___ ___ ___ ___ (numbered blanks: 14, 3, 26, 38, 24)

3. Those who followed Jesus ___ ___ ___ ___ ___ ___ ___ ___ ___ (numbered blanks: 31, 39, 5, 13)

4. Where you are baptized ___ ___ ___ ___ ___ ___ ___ ___ ___   ___ ___ ___ ___ (numbered blanks: 8, 2, 28, 12, 19, 33)

5. The age you can be baptized ___ ___ ___ ___ ___ ___   ___ ___ ___ ___ ___   ___ ___ ___ (numbered blanks: 10, 22, 9, 25, 17)

6. A gift given to you at baptism ___ ___ ___ ___   ___ ___ ___ ___ ___ (numbered blanks: 23, 20, 29, 4)

7. A book of scripture ___ ___ ___ ___   ___ ___   ___ ___ ___ ___ ___ ___ (numbered blanks: 1, 32, 35, 11, 27, 18)

8. "I hope they call me on a ____." ___ ___ ___ ___ ___ ___ ___ (numbered blanks: 7, 36, 16, 34)

"___ ___ ___ ___ ___ ___ ___   ___ ___   ___ ___ ___ ___ ___ ___ ___ ___ ___
(1 2 3 4 5 6 7   8 9   10 11 12 13 14 15 16 17 18)

___ ___ ___   ___ ___ ___   ___ ___ ___ ___ ___ ___ ___ ___ ___   ___ ___
(19 20 21   22 23 24   25 26 27 28 29 30 31 32 33   34 35)

___ ___ ___ ___" (Articles of Faith 1:4).
(36 37 38 39)

Keep the Commandments

Maze

Then Peter said unto them, repent and be baptized every one of you in the name of Jesus Christ for the remission of sins, and ye shall receive the gift of the Holy Ghost.

—Acts 2:38

Write the words that correspond with the clues. Begin with the ⋆. Read the answers on the lines beginning with number 1 to learn the words to a song about what happens when we are baptized.

rain	⋆I	with	life	I	earth	I	to
be	the	my	as	be	love	peace	want
after	Lord	light	eternal	and	God	can	again
live	want	as	right	to	best	joy	clean

1. ⋆ ____________________
2. Down 3 spaces ____________________
3. Right 1 space, up 2 spaces ____________________
4. Up 1 space, right 1 space ____________
5. 4 spaces right ____________________
6. Down 1 space, left 3 spaces ____________________
7. Down 2 spaces, left 2 spaces ____________________
8. 5 spaces right ____________________
9. Up 2 spaces, 4 spaces left ____________________
10. Up 1 space, 2 spaces right ____________________
11. Down 3 spaces, 2 spaces left ____________________
12. Up 1 space, 3 spaces left ____________________
13. Up 2 spaces ____________________
14. 6 spaces right ____________________
15. 1 space down, 1 space right ____________________
16. 2 spaces down, 3 spaces left ____________________
17. 4 spaces left, 2 spaces up ____________________
18. 1 space right ____________________
19. 2 spaces down, 4 spaces right ____________________
20. 3 spaces up, 1 space left ____________________
21. 2 spaces down, 2 spaces right ____________________
22. 2 spaces left ____________________
23. 4 spaces left, 1 space down ____________________
24. 2 spaces right, 3 spaces up ____________________
25. 2 spaces down, 3 spaces right ____________________
26. 2 spaces right ____________________

(*Children's Songbook*, 103)

PREPARE FOR BAPTISM

Letter Clue

And after this manner shall ye baptize
in my name.
—3 Nephi 11:27

• • • • • • • • • • • • • • • • •

Write the word for each definition. Then write the numbered letters below to complete a scripture about baptism. Look the scripture up when you're through.

1. The way you are baptized ___ ___ ___ ___ ___ ___ ___ ___ ___
   16 27 11 35 5

2. A talk with Heavenly Father ___ ___ ___ ___ ___ ___
   3 13 24

3. Receiving the Holy Ghost ___ ___ ___ ___ ___ ___ ___ ___ ___ ___ ___ ___
   36 30 20 15 25

4. A saving priesthood act (baptism for example) ___ ___ ___ ___ ___ ___ ___ ___ ___
   1 19 26 8 32

5. Who baptized Jesus? ___ ___ ___ ___   ___ ___ ___   ___ ___ ___ ___ ___ ___ ___
   31 23 21 4 14 22 40

6. Say you're sorry ___ ___ ___ ___ ___ ___ ___ ___ ___
   7 29 39 17 2

7. Opposite of a lie ___ ___ ___ ___ ___
   41 34 6 37

8. A book of scripture ___ ___ ___ ___ ___
   10 12 28

9. The authority to baptize ___ ___ ___ ___ ___ ___ ___ ___ ___ ___
   38 18 33 9

"You must ___ ___ ___ ___ ___ ___   ___ ___ ___   ___ ___
1 2 3 4 5 6   7 8 9   10 11

___ ___ ___ ___ ___ ___ ___ ___   ___ ___   ___ ___ ___   ___ ___ ___ ___   ___ ___
12 13 14 15 16 17 18 19   20 21   22 23 24   25 26 27 28   29 30

___ ___ ___ ___ ___ ___   ___ ___ ___ ___ ___ ___" (D&C 18:41).
31 32 33 34 35   36 37 38 39 40 41

The Lord's Way

Code

And he came into all the country about
Jordan, preaching the baptism of
repentance for the remission of sins.
—Luke 3:3

Figure out the code word and place the new word on the corresponding number in the sentence below to discover the example we should follow for baptism.

1. Jungle – ungle + opposite of off with an h in the middle ________________ A

   thanks – anks + e ________________ B   Baby – by + p + fist – f +t ______________ C

2. July – ly + deal – l ________________ D

3. Im + merci, exchange c for s + opposite of off ________________ E

4. Jelly – elly + order – er + pan – p ________________ F

"Jesus came to ____________ A ________ B ______________ C, in ______________ D long ago and was baptized by ______________ E in the River ______________ F flow" ("Baptism," *Children's Songbook*, 100).

In the Water

EZ Maze

Behold, ye shall go down and stand in
the water, and in my name shall ye
baptize them.

—3 Nephi 11:23

Follow the path through the water to reach the girl being baptized.

START

The Way We Are Baptized

Scripture Find

Each scripture below has a missing word. Choose the right word and put the correct letter on the lines below to make a word that tells how we are baptized.

1. "John did baptize in the wilderness, and preach the baptism of __________ for the remission of sins" (Mark 1:4).
   If the answer is repentance, *write the letter* **I**. *If it is* Jesus, *write the letter* **J**.
2. "I know that if ye shall ________ the Son, with full purpose of heart, ... repenting of your sins, witnessing unto the Father that ye are willing to take upon you the name of Christ, by baptism—then cometh the baptism of fire and of the Holy Ghost" (2 Nephi 31:13).
   If the answer is look to, *write the letter* **E**. *If it is* follow, *write the letter* **M**.
3. "For the gate by which ye should enter is repentance and baptism by water; and then cometh a remission of your sins by fire and by the ____________" (2 Nephi 31:17).
   If the answer is Holy Ghost, *write the letter* **M**. *If it is* son of God, *write the letter* **V**.
4. "They were desirous to be baptized as a __________ and a testimony that they were willing to serve God with all their hearts" (Mosiah 21:35).
   If the answer is example, *write the letter* **S**. *If it is* witness, *write the letter* **E**.
5. "Come and go forth, and show unto your God that ye are willing to repent of your sins and enter into a covenant with him to keep his ___________, and witness it unto him this day by going into the waters of baptism" (Alma 7:15).
   If the answer is laws, *write the letter* **W**. *If it is* commandments, *write the letter* **R**.
6. "Teach them … to understand the doctrine of repentance, faith in Christ the Son of the living God, and of baptism and the gift of the Holy Ghost by the laying on of the hands, when ______ years old" (Doctrine and Covenants 68:25).
   If the answer is eight, *write the letter* **S**. *If it is* six, *write the letter* **C**.
7. "And their _________ children need no repentance, neither baptism" (Moroni 8:11).
   If the answer is young, *write the letter* **N**. *If it is* little, *write the letter* **I**.
8. "The person who is called of God and has __________ from Jesus Christ to baptize, shall go down into the water with the person who has presented himself or herself for baptism" (Doctrine and Covenants 20:73).
   If the answer is authority, *write the letter* **O**. *If it is* permission, *write the letter* **P**.
9. "And ________ said unto them, Ye shall indeed drink of the cup that I drink of; and with the baptism that I am baptized withal shall ye be baptized" (Mark 10:39).
   If the answer is John, *write the letter* **E**. *If it is* Jesus, *write the letter* **N**.

___ ___ ___ ___ ___ ___ ___ ___ ___
1 2 3 4 5 6 7 8 9

Choose Your Words

Matching

If thou be kind to this people, and please them, and speak good words to them, they will be thy servants for ever.
—2 Chronicles 10:7

• • • • • • • • • • • • • • • • •

Complete each phrase about a good choice by matching each with words you might use. Then put the letter from the match on the blanks below (according to the matched number) to spell out someone who helps us make good choices.

1. Speak kindly	L. "I'm sorry."
2. Serve others	O. "In the name of Jesus Christ, amen."
3. Apologize	O. "May I help you?"
4. Be grateful	T. "I will change and do better."
5. Be obedient	H. "I like you."
6. Be honest	G. "Yes, Mother, I will."
7. Be prayerful	S. "And it came to pass"
8. Read the scriptures	Y. "Thank you."
9. Repent	H. "I will tell the truth."

___ ___ ___ ___   ___ ___ ___ ___ ___
1 2 3 4   5 6 7 8 9

Do As I'm Doing

Word Scramble

Wherefore, ye must press forward with
a steadfastness in Christ.
—2 Nephi 31:20

Unscramble the words below to learn ways to behave to earn blessings. Put each unscrambled word in the corresponding numbered line below.

1. sohetn
2. etur
3. hecats
4. teeolvbnen
5. uvrstuoi
6. eveible
7. ophe
8. denudre
9. stvuiuro
10. yloevl
11. oprter
12. ahopsyierwtr

"We believe in being __________ (1), __________ (2), __________ (3), __________ (4), __________ (5), and in doing good to all men; indeed, we may say that we follow the admonition of Paul—We __________ (6) all things, we __________ (7) all things, we have __________ (8) many things, and hope to be able to endure all things. If there is anything __________ (9), __________ (10), or of good __________ (11) or __________ (12), we seek after these things" (Articles of Faith 1:13).

Fruits of the Spirit

Word Search

For the fruit of the Spirit is in all goodness and righteousness and truth.
—Ephesians 5:9

Search in all directions for words that will tell you when the Holy Ghost is with you.

E	T	I	U	R	F	B	P	I	K	W	V	E
D	F	K	L	E	Q	N	O	Z	P	D	C	E
F	A	I	T	H	P	O	M	F	E	N	K	S
S	S	G	W	Y	X	E	R	L	A	C	V	S
P	B	T	O	A	V	I	U	R	C	B	A	E
I	J	O	Y	O	B	L	E	K	E	J	L	N
R	R	I	L	F	D	P	L	C	H	A	M	K
I	L	P	T	O	M	N	N	W	A	T	R	E
T	Y	C	P	E	X	H	E	M	C	Y	T	E
G	E	N	T	L	E	N	E	S	S	I	A	M
B	O	F	X	A	J	O	V	O	S	P	H	J
G	N	I	R	E	F	F	U	S	G	N	O	L

Faith
Fruit
Gentleness
Goodness
Joy
Longsuffering
Love
Meekness
Peace
Spirit
Temperance

LEAP OF FAITH

Code

I am the light of the world: he that
followeth me shall not walk in darkness
but shall have the light of life.
—John 8: 12

• • • • • • • • • • • • • • • • •

Under each letter below, place the letter that follows it in the alphabet. Continue through to the end and see an important message. For the letter Z, leap to A.

H V H K K E N K K N V F N C'R O K Z M E N Q L D

__ _____ ________ _____'__ _____ ____ ___.

Look to the Savior

Scripture Find

Look up each scripture below about choices we make and fill in the missing words (most scriptures have more than one). Add the words to the scriptures at the bottom of the puzzle over the numbers they match. To check your answers, look up the final scripture.

1. "Envy thou not the oppressor, and ____________ (13) none of ____________ (3) ways" (Proverbs 3:31).

2. "Every man seeking the interest of ____________ (10) neighbor, ____________ (6) doing all things with an eye single to the glory of God" (Doctrine and Covenants 82:19).

3. "____________ (1) unto me now therefore, O ye children, and attend to the ____________ (11) of my mouth" (Proverbs 7:24).

4. "And being made perfect, he became the author of eternal salvation ____________ (9) all them that obey him" (Hebrews 5:9).

5. "Wherefore, brethren, seek not to counsel the Lord, but to take counsel from his hand. For behold, ye yourselves know that he counseleth in wisdom, ____________ (12) in justice, and in ____________ (4) mercy, over all his works" (Jacob 4:10).

6. "He hath given ____________ (2) you that ye might know good from evil, and he hath given unto you that ye might choose ____________ (15) or death; and ye can do good and ____________ (7) restored unto that which is good, or have that which is good restored unto you; or ye can do evil, and have that which is evil restored unto you" (Helaman 14:31).

7. "Now, as you have asked, behold, I say unto you, keep my ____________ (5), and seek to bring forth and establish the cause of Zion" (Doctrine and Covenants 6:6).

8. "To others it is given to believe on their words, that they also might have ____________ (14) life if they continue ____________ (8)" (Doctrine and Covenants 46:14).

"I would that ye should look to the great Mediator, and ________ (1) ________ (2) ________ (3)

________ (4) ________ (5); ________ (6) ________ (7) ________ (8) ________ (9)

________ (10) ________ (11); ________ (12) ________ (13) ________ (14) ________ (15)"

(2 Nephi 2:28).

The Right Choice

EZ Dot

Choose the right way and be happy,
I must always choose the right.
—Children's Songbook, 160

Begin at the # sign and follow your way around back to the # sign. The object that appears will remind you to choose the right.

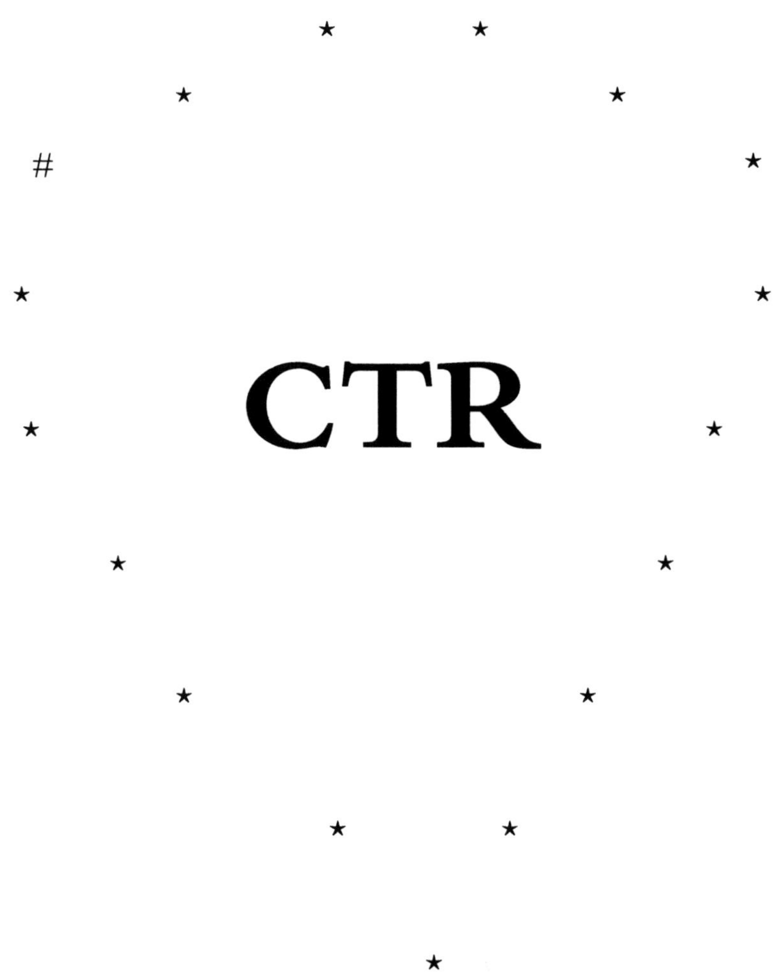

This Brings Me Joy

Code

And they are free to choose liberty
and eternal life.
—2 Nephi 2:27

• • • • • • • • • • • • • • • • •

Change each letter in the letter groups below to the letter that follows it in the alphabet. The letter Z will precede the letter A.

BGNNRD SGD QHFGS VZX ZMC AD GZOOX. H LTRS ZKVZXR BGNNRD SGD QHFGS.

("Choose the Right," *Children's Songbook*, 161)

WORD OF WISDOM CHOICES

Logic

I have warned you, and forewarn you,
by giving unto you this word of wisdom
by revelation.

—D&C 89:4

• • • • • • • • • • • • • • • • •

Each child in the Walstrom family (the brothers were Don and David and the sisters were Cathy and Mary) chose one part of the Word of Wisdom to present in Family Home Evening and each had a different activity to present the principle. From the clues below, can you find how each child presented part of the Word of Wisdom (song, game, puzzle, or video)? Cross out the choices in the boxes according to the clues to reveal the answers.

1. David did not give the "tobacco is not good for man" message and Mary didn't present the game.
2. Either Don or Cathy showed a video (which was not about "hot drinks are not for the body").
3. Neither of the brothers presented the game or the message about "health in the navel."
4. One of the sisters chose the puzzle and the other sister had the message about eating "every herb and fruit."

Name				Principle	Activity			
David	Don	Cathy	Mary	"Tobacco is not good for man."	Game	Puzzle	Song	Video
David	Don	Cathy	Mary	"Hot drinks are not for the body."	Game	Puzzle	Song	Video
David	Don	Cathy	Mary	"Health in the navel"	Game	Puzzle	Song	Video
David	Don	Cathy	Mary	"Every herb and fruit"	Game	Puzzle	Song	Video

YOUR BEST CHOICE

Letter Clue

You must study it out in your mind;
then you must ask me if it be right.
—Doctrine and Covenants 9:8

• • • • • • • • • • • • • • • • •

Write the word for each definition. Then write the numbered letters below to complete a scripture about an important choice. Look it up when you're through!

1. Telling the truth shows ___ ___ ___ ___ ___ ___ ___
18 3 36 32 16
2. Talks with Heavenly Father ___ ___ ___ ___ ___ ___ ___
34 7 22 13
3. A feeling of love and respect ___ ___ ___ ___ ___ ___ ___ ___ ___
28 35 6 39
4. The opposite of wrong ___ ___ ___ ___ ___
42 24 2 10
5. The opposite of illness ___ ___ ___ ___ ___ ___
11 31 40
6. A book of scripture ___ ___ ___ ___ ___ ___ ___ ___ ___ ___ ___ ___
41 19 8 4 29 20
7. Parents, children, and grandparents ___ ___ ___ ___ ___ ___
12 26 21
8. Sacred promises ___ ___ ___ ___ ___ ___ ___ ___ ___
1 30 33 37 27
9. Full of gratitude ___ ___ ___ ___ ___ ___ ___ ___
38 15 9 25
10. The Lord's law of health ___ ___ ___ ___ ___ ___ ___ ___ ___ ___ ___ ___ ___
17 43 23 5 14

"___ ___ ___ ___ ___ ___ ___ ___ ___ ___ ___ ___ ___ ___ ___ ___ ___ ___
1 2 3 4 5 6 7 8 9 10 11 12 13 14 15 16 17 18

___ ___ ___ ___ ___ ___ ___ ___ ___ ___ ___ ___ ___ but as for me and my house, we will
19 20 21 22 23 24 25 26 27 28 29 30 31

___ ___ ___ ___ ___ ___ ___ ___ ___ ___ ___ ___" (Joshua 24:15).
32 33 34 35 36 37 38 39 40 41 42 43

Shine Your Light

Maze

And the light which shineth, which giveth you light, is through him who enlighteneth your eyes, which is the same light that quickeneth your understanding.
—Doctrine and Covenants 88:11

Write the words that correspond with the clues. Begin with the ⋆. Read the answers on the lines beginning with number 1 to learn the words to a scripture.

love	want	see	glorify	and	your	that
⋆Therefore	child	going	and	good	people	he
is	your	may	in	me	light	your
works	this	so	earth	they	temple	someday
let	here	God	to	sent	given	heaven
shine	who	has	Father	there	before	me

1. ⋆ ________________
2. Down 3 spaces ________________
3. Right 1 space, up 2 spaces ________________
4. 4 spaces right ________________
5. Down 1 space, left 3 spaces ________________
6. Down 2 spaces, left 2 spaces ________________
7. 5 spaces right ________________
8. Up 2 spaces, 4 spaces left ________________
9. Up 2 spaces, 4 spaces right ________________
10. Up 1 space, 1 space right ________________
11. Down 3 spaces, 2 spaces left ________________
12. Up 1 space, 2 spaces left ________________
13. Up 2 spaces ________________
14. 3 spaces right ________________
15. 1 space down, 1 space left ________________
16. 2 spaces down, 4 spaces left ________________
17. 4 spaces right, 3 spaces up ________________
18. 1 space left ________________
19. 2 spaces down, 3 spaces right ________________
20. 3 spaces down, 3 spaces left ________________
21. 2 spaces left ________________
22. 3 spaces up, 1 space left ________________
23. 3 spaces right ________________
24. 3 spaces right, 2 spaces down ________________

(3 Nephi 12:16)

AMAZING FAITH

Maze

This is my beloved Son. Hear Him.
—Joseph Smith History 1:1

Write the words that correspond with the clues below. Begin with the ⋆.

⋆We	on	mission	temple	honor	and	ponder	Heavenly	good	every
Savior	baptism	voice	God	man	now	for	Happiness	in	unto
joy	love	read	gift	joy	kind	Christ	serving	day	yea
believe	always	in	the	in	me	follow	testimony	kind	thy
courage	Teach	there	Spirit	Eternal	Father	on	Ghost	love	study
family	every	listen	happy	Jesus	pray	Us	sacrament	pray	happy
in	prayer	hope	Choose	will	and	Holy	and	joy	faith
Jesus	faith	duty	love	Son	faith	our	counselor	serve	trust
child	His	plan	word	holy	unto	seek	covenants	good	peace
happy	honest	live	study	keep	Jesus	peace	Father	help	the

1. Begin at⋆: ________________
2. 3 spaces down ________________
3. 2 spaces right ________________
4. 2 spaces up, 1 space right ________________
5. 2 spaces down ________________
6. 1 space down, 1 space right ________________
7. 1 space right ________________
8. 2 spaces down ________________
9. 5 spaces left ________________
10. 2 spaces down, 1 space right ________________
11. 3 spaces right, 1 space up ________________
12. 1 space right, 2 spaces down ________________
13. 1 space right, 7 spaces up ________________
14. 4 spaces down, 1 space right ________________
15. 1 space right, 5 spaces up ________________
16. 1 space right, 8 spaces down ________________
17. 3 spaces left, 3 spaces up ________________
18. 2 spaces up, 1 space right ________________

(Articles of Faith 1:1)

Believe in the Lord Jesus Christ

Letter Clue

Believe on the Lord Jesus Christ, and
thou shalt be saved.
—Acts 16:31

• • • • • • • • • • • • • • • • •

Write the word for each definition. Then write the numbered letters below to complete a line from a song about faith. Look it up when you're through.

1. Jesus ___ ___ ___ ___ ___ ___ the Savior
   27 12 23 33

2. Something you say when you've hurt someone's feelings ___ ___ ___ ___ ___
   15 35 21

3. We should try to ___ ___ ___ ___ ___ ___the prophet.
   5 10 8

4. A talk with Heavenly Father ___ ___ ___ ___ ___ ___
   6 26 37 19

5. The first ordinance of the church ___ ___ ___ ___ ___ ___ ___
   20 34 1 9 16

6. Articles of Faith begin, "We ___ ___ ___ ___ ___ ___ ___ . . ."
   3 11 30 22

7. A special house of the Lord ___ ___ ___ ___ ___ ___
   25 31 18 13

8. To whom we pray ___ ___ ___ ___ ___ ___ ___ ___ ___ ___ ___ ___ ___ ___
   2 32 4 14 29 28

9. The day we go to church ___ ___ ___ ___ ___ ___
   24 7 36 17

"Faith is knowing ___ ___ ___ ___ ___ ___ ___ ___ ___ ___ ___ ___ ___ ___ ___
1 2 3 4 5 6 7 8 9 10 11 12 13 14 15

___ ___ ___ ___ ___ ___ ___ ___ ___ ___ ___ ___ ___ ___ ___ ___ ___ ___
16 17 18 19 20 21 22 23 24 25 26 27 28 29 30 31 32 33

___ ___ ___ ___" (*Children's Songbook*, 215).
34 35 36 37

FAITH IS . . .

Missing Letter Words

Yea, he that repenteth and exerciseth faith, and bringeth forth good works, and prayeth continually without ceasing—unto such is given to know the mysteries of God.

—Alma 26:22

Every other letter is missing from the words below. The letters are listed in alphabetical order in the box beside the phrase. Replace each letter to find phrases that tell about faith. The scripture references have the answers if you get stuck.

1. g __ a __ n __ f __ u __ t __ r __ s __ e __ (Matthew 17:20)

a d d e i m o r s

2. __ h __ f __ i __ h __ a __ h __ a __ e __ t __ e __ (Luke 7:50).

a d e h h s t t t v y

3. __ h __ l __ r __ n __ f __ o __ (Galatians 3:36).

c d d e g i o

4. __ b __ y __ n __ o __ s __ r __ e (Alma 57:21).

a b d e e o v

5. f __ i __ h __ o __ e __ e __ l __ d (D&C 46:19).

a a b e h t t

6. __ i __ n __ f __ l __ o __ t __ o __ e __ h __ t __ e __ i __ v __ (D&C 63:9)

a b e e g h l l o s s s t w

First Principle

Code

Teach them to humble themselves and be meek and lowly in heart; teach them to withstand every temptation of the devil, with their faith on the Lord Jesus Christ.
—Alma 37:33

Using the code circle below, match the shape with the letter closest to it. Write the letters above each clue shape to reveal a scripture concerning an important truth about faith.

"We believe that the first principles and ordinances of the gospel are: . . . "

(Article of Faith 1:4)

Have Faith

Scripture Find

• • • • • • • • • • • • • • • • •

Look up each scripture about faith below and fill in the missing words (most scriptures have more than one). Add the words to the scripture at the bottom of the puzzle over the numbers they match. To check your answer, look up the final scripture.

1. "And according to his faith there was __________ (4) mighty change wrought in his heart. Behold I say unto you that this is all __________ (19)" (Alma 5:12).

2. "And the Lord said unto him: Because of thy faith thou hast __________ (16) that I shall take upon me flesh and blood; and never has man come before me with such exceeding faith as thou hast; __________ (11) were it __________ (1) so ye could not have seen my finger" (Ether 3:9).

3. "Wherefore, ______ (9) may also have __________ (10), and be partakers of the gift, if ye will but __________ (3) faith" (Ether 12:9).

4. "And Christ truly said unto our fathers: If ye have faith ye can do all __________ (12) __________ (17) __________ (14) expedient unto me" (Moroni 10:23).

5. "Remember that without faith you can do nothing; therefore ask in faith. Trifle not with these __________ (8); do __________ (15) ask for that __________ (13) you ought not" (Doctrine and Covenants 8:10).

6. "And he commandeth all men that they must repent, and be baptized in his name, having __________ (5) faith in the Holy One of Israel, or they cannot be saved in the kingdom _____ (7) God" (2 Nephi 9:23).

7. "And a portion of that Spirit dwelleth in me, which giveth me __________ (6), and also power according ___ (2) my faith and desires which _______ (18) in God" (Alma 18:35).

" And now as I said concerning faith—faith is __________ (1) __________ (2) __________ (3) __________ (4) __________ (5) __________ (6) __________ (7) __________ (8); therefore if ye have faith __________ (9) __________ (10) __________ (11) __________ (12) __________ (13) __________ (14) __________ (15) __________ (16), __________ (17) __________ (18) __________ (19)" (Alma 32:21).

Perfect Faith

Scripture Find

• • • • • • • • • • • • • • • • •

Each scripture below has two word choices. Choose the correct word in the scripture and write the word on the numbered line at the bottom of the page to tell about a great promise that the Lord gives us when we have faith.

1. "Wherefore, let him do as the Spirit of the living God ***commandeth*** (or) ***charged*** him, whether upon the land or upon the waters, as it remaineth with me to do hereafter" (Doctrine & Covenants 61:28).
2. "Therefore, what manner of ***people*** (or) ***men*** ought ye to be?" (3 Nephi 27:27).
3. "***Repent*** (or) ***rejoice***: yea for the kingdom of heaven is at hand" (Matthew 3:2).
4. "Then they that gladly received his word were ***baptized*** (or) ***blessed***: and the same day there were added unto them about three thousand souls" (Acts 2:41).
5. "Father, glorify thy ***name*** (or) ***word***. Then came there a voice from heaven, saying, I have both glorified it, and will glorify it again" (John 12:28).
6. "Be ***perfect*** (or) ***patient***, be of good comfort, be of one mind, live in peace; and the God of love and peace shall be with you" (2 Corinthians 13:11).
7. "And beside this, giving all diligence, add to your ***faith*** (or) ***patience*** virtue; and to virtue knowledge" (2 Peter 1:5).
8. "Wherefore the law is holy and the commandment ***holy*** (or) ***pure***, and just, and good" (Romans 7:12).
9. "Wherefore, I speak unto all the house of ***Israel*** (or) ***Jacob***, if it so be that they should obtain these things" (1 Nephi 19:19).
10. "And he said to the woman, Thy faith hath ***saved*** (or) ***delivered*** thee; go in peace" (Luke 7:50).
11. "But before ye seek for riches, seek ye for the ***church*** (or) ***kingdom*** of God" (Jacob 2:18).
12. "I say unto you, can ye look up to ***God*** (or) ***Heaven*** at that day with a pure heart and clean hands: I say unto you, can you look up, having the image of God engraven upon your countenances?" (Alma 5:19).

"And he ____________ (1) all ____________ (2) that they must ____________ (3), and be _____ (4) in his ____________ (5), having ____________ (6) ____________ (7) in the ____________ (8) One of ____________ (9), or they cannot be ____________ (10) in the ____________ (11) of ____________ (12)"

(2 Nephi 9:23).

Power from Above

Matching

Behold it was by faith that they of old
were called after the holy order of God.
—Ether 12:10

• • • • • • • • • • • • • • • • •

Match the following scriptural leaders with the faith action. Place the letter of each clue's answer on the corresponding line below for the answer of how they had to accomplish their task.

1. Limhi	E. Sealed up the gold plates in the Hill Cumorah (Moroni 10:2)
2. Brother of Jared	U. Righteous leader of 2000 warriors in battle (Alma 53:17–18)
3. Nephi	U. Built a ship while the Lord showed him how (1 Nephi 18:1–4)
4. Ammon	G. Prayed all night (Enos 1:4)
5. Anti-Nephi-Lehis	O. Asked the Lord to touch the stones to make light (Ether 3:4)
6. Enos	L. Prayed and fasted for his son (Alma 27:14)
7. Moroni	C. Followed Gideon's plan to escape (Mosiah 22:9–12)
8. Lehi	S. Converted by the teachings of Ammon (Alma 18:36, 40)
9. Helaman	Y. Testified of truth and died by fire (Mosiah 17:20)
10. Lamoni	A. Buried their weapons of war (Alma 24:12–19)
11. Alma the Elder	O. Saw a vision to leave Jerusalem (1 Nephi 1:6–15)
12. Abinidi	R. Saved King Lamoni's flock (Alma 17:26–39)

___	___	___	___	___	___	___	___	___	___	___	___
1	2	3	4	5	6	7	8	9	10	11	12

QUIET FRIEND

Hidden Message

Howebeit when he, the Spirit of truth, is come, he will guide you into all truth: for he shall not speak of himself; but whatsoever he shall hear, that shall he speak: and he will shew you things to come.

—John 16:13

In the box below, color the space of any words that have the letters **b f j p q r x z**.

Circle the remaining words and read from left to right an important message about a special friend that will help you.

pray	Listen	to	quick	place	the	flag	of	still	by
small	staff	read	voice	baptize	listen	are	quiet	listen	when
friend	you	cab	play	boy	have	quit	peace	pace	to
make	excite	a	water	absent	prayer	be	choice	perfect	joy
blessing	amaze	for	he	try	earth	will	fill	above	over
bring	guide	by	early	you	over	girl	pray	always	peace

(*Children's Songbook*, 107)

Words of Faith

Crossword

Yea, it will strengthen your faith: for ye will say I know that this is a good seed; for behold it sprouteth and beginneth to grow.

—Alma 32:30

The scriptures teach us about what faith is and what it is not. Use the scripture reference next to each clue if you need a hint. When you have solved the puzzle, unscramble the highlighted letters (beginning with the highlighted letter in clue number 9) to discover something you need in order to have faith.

Across

1. A talk with Heavenly Father (D&C 104:79)
5. Move your feet (2 Corinthians 5:7)
8. The Savior—2 words (Articles of Faith 1:4)
9. Having a remission of sins (Mark 2:5)
10. Your address is where you ___ (Romans 1:17)

Down

2. To request (1 Nephi 15:11)
3. Opposite of faith; to not believe (Matt 21:21)
4. To gradually become greater (Luke 17:5)
5. Scriptures—3 words (Romans 10:17)
6. Trusting in something (Moroni 7:26)
7. Gaining knowledge (D&C 109:7)

___ ___ ___ ___ ___ ___ ___ ___ ___ (See Romans 16:26)

Walk with Faith

EZ Maze

For we walk by faith, not by sight.
—2 Corinthians 5:7

START

FINISH

A Mother's Work

Word Search

And to be a joyful mother of children.
Praise ye the Lord.
—Psalms 113:9

• • • • • • • • • • • • • • • • •

Find the words about things our mothers do for us in the word search maze below. A few can be found backwards and diagonally, as well as up and down and side to side. Draw a line through each word as you find it. When you finish, put the unused letters on the blanks below (reading them from left to right), and find out how one song describes our mothers.

P	E	S	E	V	I	R	D	L	C
E	R	S	I	O	N	B	R	O	I
D	N	I	K	N	G	H	O	V	T
P	Y	C	A	N	G	K	D	I	S
L	R	J	O	Y	F	U	L	N	T
O	D	A	V	U	R	E	A	G	E
B	N	L	Y	Y	R	E	I	S	A
N	U	R	S	E	L	A	A	M	C
Y	A	S	M	C	R	O	G	D	H
T	L	H	Y	E	R	F	D	E	E
E	A	H	E	L	P	F	U	L	S
O	B	E	D	I	E	N	T	L	R

Busy
Cleans
Cook
Drives
Encourages
Helpful
Joyful
Kind
Laundry
Loving
Nurse
Obedient
Prayerful
Read
Sing
Teaches

"A _

_ _ _ _ _ _ _ _ _ _ _ _ _ _ _ _ _ _ _ _" (*Children's Songbook*, 203).

Family Home Evening Assignments

Logic

Teach the children of men the things
which I have put into your hands by the
power of my Spirit.
—Doctrine and Covenants 43:15

When the Barnes family had a Family Home Evening, each child was given an assignment, but somebody lost the list. From the clues below, can you help them remember the assignments they were given? Cross out assignments according to the clues, and you should discover the answers.

1. Neither Jeannie nor Thomas prepared the treat or chose the game.
2. The child who chose the scripture has a name that begins with a letter that appears in the alphabet before H.
3. A girl made the treat and a boy chose the prayer.
4. Benjamin did not offer the prayer or prepare the lesson.

Name	Assignment				
Benjamin	Scripture	Prayer	Lesson	Game	Treat
Cindy	Scripture	Prayer	Lesson	Game	Treat
Jeannie	Scripture	Prayer	Lesson	Game	Treat
Michael	Scripture	Prayer	Lesson	Game	Treat
Thomas	Scripture	Prayer	Lesson	Game	Treat

FAMILY TIES

Word Scramble

Shall all the families of the earth be
blessed, even with the blessings of the
Gospel, which are the blessings of
salvation, even of life eternal.
—Abraham 2:11

Unscramble the following words on the left and match them to the clues on the right.

STEISR __ __ __ __ __ **R**	Mother of my mom
REFAHT __ __ **T** __ __ __	Head of the household
EUCLN __ __ __ **L** __	My mother's brother
ANGDPRA __ __ __ __ __ __ __	Father of my dad
MGDARAN __ __ **A** __ __ __ __	Married to Father
EROBTRH __ __ __ __ __ **E** __	A female sibling
OTMRHE __ __ __ __ **E** __	My father's sister
TANU __ __ **N** __	Opposite of sister

Unscramble the words in bold on the lines above for a message about family ties.

__ __ __ __ __ __ __

HEAVEN ON EARTH

Maze

May the Lord Jesus Christ grant that
their prayers may be answered.
—Mormon 9:37

Write the words that correspond with the clues below. Begin with ⋆pray.

⋆Pray	joy	that	faith	and	love	see	do	name	man
happy	eternal	temples	peace	always	care	Father	trust	may	that
your	duty	share	clean	find	spirit	patience	always	what	kind
kind	in	do	pray	your	listen	good	and	we	children
in	child	be	sing	heart	in	share	be	my	day
day	your	grateful	joy	love	praise	do	unto	smart	good
good	plan	smart	love	to	be	man	families	look	may
holy	follow	families	unto	the	people	the	river	Christ	keep
keep	place	true	that	going	you	blessed	baptize	listen	duty
wives	honor	humble	and	holy	kind	father	our	true	blessed

1. ⋆________
2. 1 space right, 3 spaces down_______
3. 3 spaces right________
4. 4 spaces down, 2 spaces left __________
5. 1 space right ___________
6. 3 spaces right___________
7. 6 spaces up ___________
8. 2 spaces left ___________
9. 3 spaces down, 1 space right____________
10. 3 spaces right
11. 4 spaces up
12. 6 spaces left __________
13. 2 spaces down, 2 spaces left ____________
14. 7 spaces down ___________
15. 3 spaces right__________
16. 4 spaces up, 2 spaces left _____________
17. 8 spaces right, 2 spaces up__________
18. 3 spaces down ____________
19. 4 spaces left ____________
20. 3 spaces down, 4 spaces right_____________ (3 Nephi 18:21)

Our House

Word Scramble

Visit the house of each member,
exhorting them to pray vocally and in
secret and attend to all family duties.
—Doctrine and Covenants 20:51

• • • • • • • • • • • • • • • • •

Unscramble the words below to discover those things that the Lord wants in our homes and write each word on the numbered lines in the scripture below.

1. AERRPY
2. IAGTFSN
3. AIHFT
4. AEIGLNNR
5. OGYLR
6. EODRR

"Establish a house, even a house of ______________ (1), a house of ______________ (2), a house of ______________ (3), a house of ______________ (4), a house of ______________ (5), a house of ______________ (6), a house of God" (Doctrine and Covenants 88:119).

Song in My Heart

Matching

I will praise the name of God with
a song.
—Psalms 69:30

Match the following phrases of the Primary songs with the title of the song in which they belong.

1. Teach me all that I must do
2. Teaching me how to trust and obey
3. Live like His Son
4. He knows I will follow him
5. Then we learn to know each other
6. And we sing as we go
7. I'll prepare most carefully
8. He hears and answers me
9. They love us and so you see
10. With branches by the dozen

A. The Family (*Children's Songbook*, 194)
B. He Sent His Son (*Children's Songbook*, 34)
C. I Have a Family Tree (*Children's Songbook*, 199)
D. When We're Helping (*Children's Songbook*, 198)
E. A Happy Family (*Children's Songbook*, 198)
F. I Pray in Faith (*Children's Songbook*, 14)
G. I Feel My Savior's Love (*Children's Songbook*, 74)
H. Love Is Spoken Here (*Children's Songbook*, 190)
I. I Am a Child of God (*Children's Songbook*, 2)
J. Families Can Be Together Forever (*Children's Songbook*, 188)

Together Forever

Scripture Find

• • • • • • • • • • • • • • • • •

Look up the scriptures and write in the missing words above the number in the scripture at the bottom to discover an important teaching about families. Search out the final scripture when you're through.

1. "And Jesus looking upon them saith, With men __9__ is impossible, but not with God: for with God all things are __10__" (Mark 10:27).
2. "Be determined in one mind and __5__ one heart, __15__ in all things, that ye may not come down into captivity" (2 Nephi 1:21).
3. "Behold, I am he who was prepared from the foundation of the world to redeem my people. Behold, I am Jesus Christ. I am the Father and the Son. In me shall all mankind have life, and that __16__, even they who shall believe on my name; and they shall become my sons and my daughters" (Ether 3:14).
4. "And it shall be given thee, also, to __8__ a selection of __1__ hymns, as it shall be given thee, which is pleasing unto me, to be had in my church" (Doctrine and Covenants 25:11).
5. "And again, every person who belongeth __13__ this church of Christ, shall observe to keep all the commandments and __4__ of the church" (Doctrine and Covenants 42:78).
6. " __11__ therein are the keys of the __6__ priesthood ordained, that you may receive honor and glory" (Doctrine and Covenants 124:34).
7. " __3__ this shall be our covenant—that we will walk in all the __2__ of the Lord" (Doctrine and Covenants 136:4).
8. "Foreshadowing the great work to __14__ done in the __7__ of the Lord in the dispensation of the fulness of times, for the redemption of the dead, and the sealing of the children to their parents, lest the whole earth be smitten with a curse and utterly wasted at his coming" (Doctrine and Covenants 138:48).
9. "And in that day Adam blessed God and was filled, and began to prophesy concerning all the __12__ of the earth, saying: Blessed be the name of God, for because of my transgression my eyes are opened, and in this life I shall have joy, and again in the flesh I shall see God" (Moses 5:10).

"________ ________ ________ ________ . . . ________
1 2 3 4 5

________ ________ ________ ________ ________ . . .
6 7 8 9 10

________ ________ ________ ________ ________
11 12 13 14 15

________" ("The Family: A Proclamation to the World," paragraph 3).
16

Who Am I?

Hidden Message

The Spirit itself beareth witness with our spirit, that we are the children of God.

—Romans 8:16

Color in each space that has a letter that rhymes with "me," except C, D, and G. In the remaining spaces you will discover a special message.

P	E	I	V	E	P	Z	T
V	Z	T	A	M	B	P	E
T	P	Z	E	A	T	E	Z
V	Z	C	H	I	L	D	T
B	P	E	O	F	T	V	E
E	V	T	G	O	D	P	T

One Eternal Round

Crossword

A new commandment I give unto you,
That ye lone another; as I have
loved you.
—John 13:34

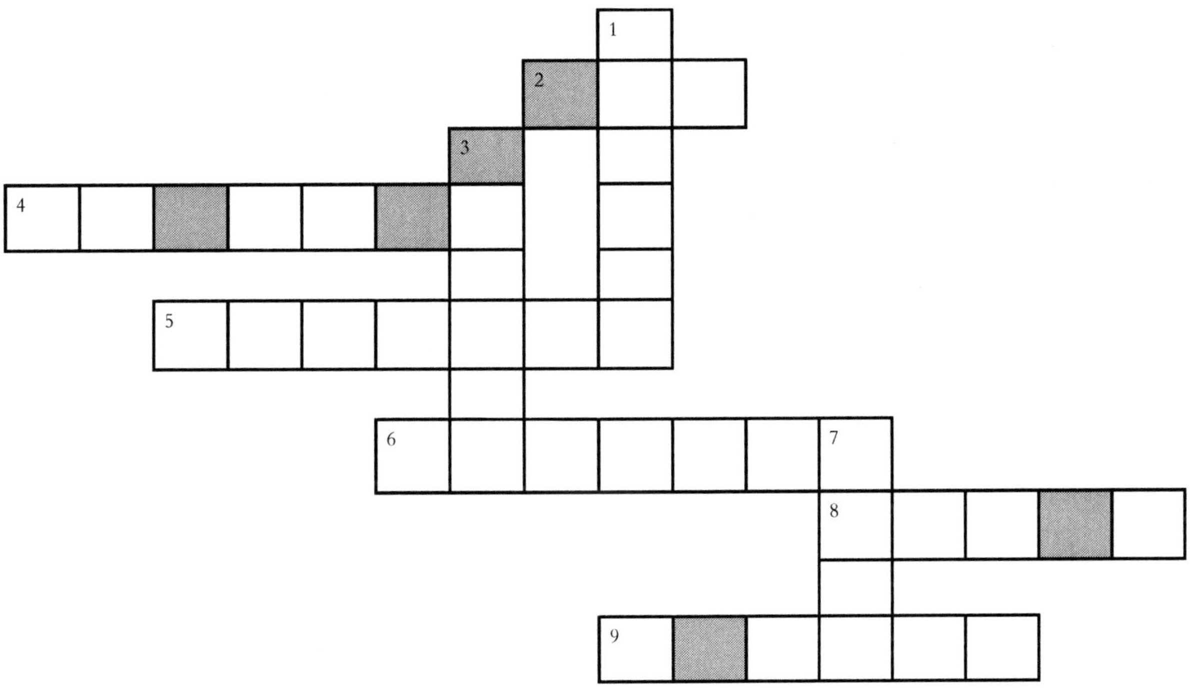

Across
2. Opposite of me
4. Married to Grandpa
5. A boy sibling
6. Your mother's father
8. Your mother's brother
9. Opposite of brother

Down
1. Your mom
3. Your dad
7. Your dad's sister

Unscramble the letters in the shaded boxes to find out what is forever when we follow God's plan.

___ ___ ___ ___ ___ ___

Signs of Home

EZ Maze

I want to do just what is best each and every day.
—Children's Songbook, 197

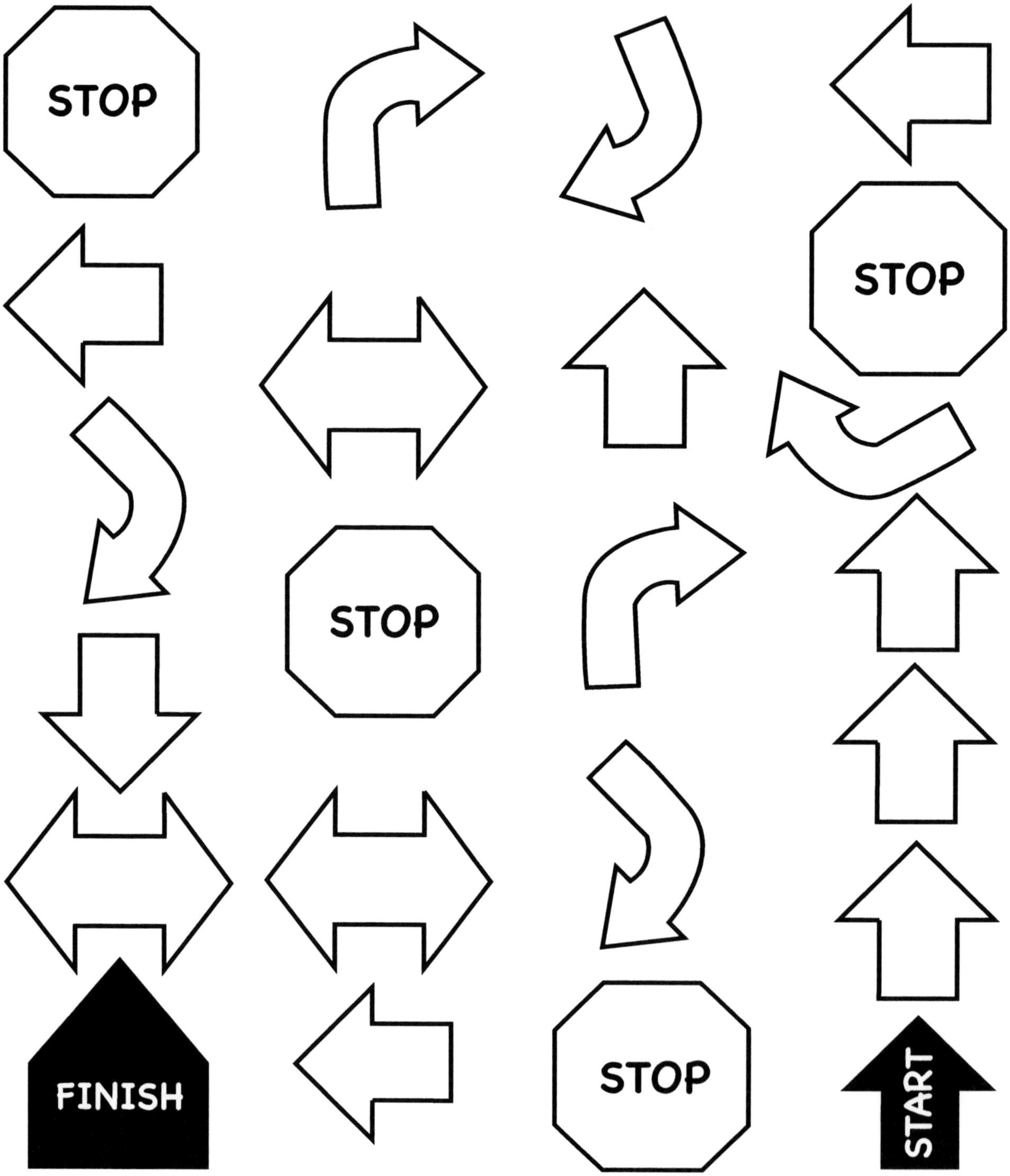

Are We Willing?

Scripture Find

Look up the scriptures and fill in the missing words. Write the underlined words in each scripture on the lines below to discover how we can follow Jesus. Search out the final scripture when you're through.

1. "And he that will not take up his cross and ________ (3) me, and keep my ________________ (13), the same shall not be saved" (Doctrine and Covenants 56:2).

2. "Wherefore, my beloved brethren, I know that if ye shall follow the Son, . . . with real intent, repenting of your sins, witnessing unto the __________ (16) that ye are ___________ (9) to take upon you the name of Christ, by baptism—behold, then shall ye receive the Holy Ghost" (2 Nephi 31:13).

3. "Remember ______ (15) sabbath day, to ________ (11) it holy" (Mosiah 13:16).

4. "And if ye do always remember me ye _____ (7) have my Spirit ____ (10) be with you" (3 Nephi 18:11).

5. "And no unclean thing _____ (1) enter into his kingdom; therefore nothing entereth into his rest ________ (5) it be those who have washed their garments in my blood, because of their faith, and the repentance of all their sins, and their faithfulness unto the end" (3 Nephi 27:19).

6. "O then ye unbelieving, turn ye unto the Lord; cry mightily unto the Father in the name of ____________ (4), that perhaps ye may ______ (8) found spotless, pure, fair, and white, having been cleansed by ______ (12) blood of the Lamb, at that great and last day" (Mormon 9:6).

7. "Wherefore, _____ (6) search the prophets, and _____ (2) have many revelations and the spirit ______ (14) prophecy; and having all these witnesses we obtain a hope, and our faith becometh unshaken" (Jacob 4:6).

"And he said unto the children of men: Follow thou me. Wherefore, my beloved brethren,

_________ (1) _________ (2) _________ (3) _________ (4) _________ (5) _________ (6) _________ (7)

_________ (8) _________ (9) _________ (10) _________ (11) _________ (12) _________ (13) _________ (14)

_________ (15) _________ (16)" (2 Nephi 31:10).

Covenant Challenge

Code

And I will make my covenant between
me and thee.
—Genesis 17:2

• • • • • • • • • • • • • • • • •

Discover the counting pattern in the code below. Use the code to fill in the words of the scripture. A letter has the same number throughout the quotation. This scripture tells us what we will be called after we have made the covenant of baptism. Search out the scripture when you're through.

5		15				
A	B	C	D	E	F	H

						70
I	L	M	N	O	R	S

T	U	V	W	Y

"
5 55 20   55 60 90   10 25 15 5 80 70 25   60 30

75 35 25   15 60 85 25 55 5 55 75   90 35 40 15 35

95 25   35 5 85 25   50 5 20 25   95 25

70 35 5 45 45   10 25   15 5 45 45 25 20   75 35 25

15 35 40 45 20 65 25 55   60 30   15 35 65 40 70 75 "

(Mosiah 5:7).

His Only Begotten Son

Letter Clue

Hearken ye to these words. Behold, I am
Jesus Christ, the Savior of the world.
—Doctrine and Covenants 43:34

• • • • • • • • • • • • • • • • •

Write the word for each definition. Then write the numbered letters below to complete a scripture about an important choice. Look it up when you're through.

1. Trusting Heavenly Father's promises ___(47) ___(31) ___(22) ___ ___(2)

2. The act of doing what you are asked ___(5) ___(10) ___(16) ___(29) ___(42) ___(33) ___(20) ___ ___(48)

3. A warm feeling you have for your family ___(45) ___(26) ___(7) ___(36)

4. True and loyal ___(15) ___(39) ___ ___(19) ___ ___(43) ___(17)

5. To whom we pray ___(21) ___(8) ___ ___(32) ___(14) ___ ___(38) ___   ___ ___ ___ ___(30) ___(11) ___(37)

6. Opposite of falsehood ___(41) ___(9) ___(27) ___ ___(18)

7. To help others ___(24) ___(6) ___ ___(35) ___

8. Special gifts from Heavenly Father ___ ___(12) ___(34) ___ ___(40) ___(46) ___ ___(44) ___(4)

9. Baptism color ___(1) ___(25) ___(13) ___ ___

10. Our kind of bodies on earth ___(23) ___(3) ___ ___ ___ ___(28)

"For God so loved the world, that he gave His only begotten Son, that . . .

___(1) ___(2) ___(3) ___(4) ___(5) ___(6) ___(7) ___(8) ___(9)   ___(10) ___(11) ___(12) ___(13) ___(14) ___(15) ___(16) ___(17) ___(18)

___(19) ___(20)   ___(21) ___(22) ___(23)   ___(24) ___(25) ___(26) ___(27) ___(28) ___(29) . . . ___(30) ___(31) ___(32) ___(33)

___(34) ___(35) ___(36) ___(37) ___(38) ___(39) ___(40) ___(41) ___(42) ___(43) ___(44)   ___(45) ___(46) ___(47) ___(48)" (John 3:16).

JESUS SAID

Missing Letter Words

Hearken ye to these words. Behold, I am
Jesus Christ, the Savior of the world.
—Doctrine and Covenants 43:34

• • • • • • • • • • • • • • • • •

Every other letter is missing from the phrases below. The letters are listed in alphabetical order in the box beside the phrase. Replace each letter to find words that tell what Jesus said about following Him. The scripture reference will help if you get stuck.

1. __ b __ y __ h __ c __ m __ a __ d __ e __ t __ (Deuteronomy 11:27) | e e m m n n o o s t |

2. g __ v __ h __ e __ __ o __ h __ p __ o __ h __ t __ (Doctrine and Covenants 1:14) | d e e e e i p r s t t |

3. l __ a __ n __ f __ e (Doctrine and Covenants 19:23) | e m o r |

4. s __ a __ c __ t __ e __ c __ i __ t __ r __ s (John 5:39) | e e h h p r r s u |

5. __ r __ y t __ t __ e __ a __ h __ r (Moroni 4:2) | a e f h o p t |

O Lord, My Redeemer

Word Search

For I know that my redeemer liveth.
—Job 19:25

Search in all directions for the different names we use to refer to our Savior, Jesus Christ.

O	N	L	Y	B	E	G	O	T	T	E	N	S	O	N	D	E	R	M	G	I	L	O	P	S
Q	H	I	L	P	M	J	H	G	E	D	S	C	G	H	H	F	N	M	O	I	U	L	M	M
M	B	R	E	A	D	O	F	L	I	F	E	W	N	O	I	U	H	Z	S	J	H	Y	E	O
H	Y	E	H	R	E	E	J	L	I	G	H	T	O	F	T	H	E	W	O	R	L	D	S	N
O	O	M	Y	J	O	Y	H	A	P	P	Y	N	H	R	U	L	P	M	N	N	B	B	S	N
Q	U	E	T	T	G	O	I	K	N	D	L	R	O	W	E	H	T	F	O	T	H	G	I	L
T	G	E	S	O	E	E	J	H	I	M	N	Y	L	G	O	O	D	D	F	N	M	C	A	F
U	O	D	K	I	U	J	H	E	G	M	C	C	Y	X	U	N	I	G	G	M	O	M	H	A
N	O	E	L	A	K	P	O	O	S	L	E	E	O	Y	E	R	F	T	O	M	N	B	V	O
K	D	R	V	M	M	L	C	I	N	U	X	I	N	Z	Y	U	J	N	D	D	E	R	R	D
Z	S	K	I	H	B	V	C	C	D	E	S	B	E	S	A	A	W	Q	W	B	N	K	N	U
T	H	H	I	T	L	K	J	B	V	H	G	C	G	H	S	H	U	S	D	I	E	E	R	S
Y	E	K	L	A	M	B	O	F	G	O	D	L	H	J	G	F	L	G	N	P	I	L	K	O
I	P	J	J	I	N	M	Y	T	G	J	O	P	L	R	J	I	Z	N	R	R	S	H	E	M
M	H	W	O	N	O	R	T	H	E	L	M	R	B	T	I	R	Y	I	F	I	A	H	M	A
Y	E	T	E	R	J	E	H	O	V	A	H	O	N	L	K	S	S	K	N	G	E	L	O	R
S	R	B	S	P	L	A	R	O	R	L	R	C	O	U	F	T	T	F	H	T	X	E	E	R
E	D	E	A	A	C	E	A	T	N	E	J	K	H	E	P	B	Y	O	N	M	E	P	L	O
T	T	T	V	F	U	L	A	A	T	D	E	R	M	L	G	O	E	G	R	E	M	E	E	L
R	F	U	I	L	D	O	Q	S	O	I	N	M	A	N	N	R	R	N	X	I	P	I	N	E
S	A	V	O	L	O	U	A	R	A	S	T	O	P	L	T	N	N	I	L	S	L	I	N	S
B	O	L	R	E	E	M	M	A	N	U	E	L	S	S	K	Y	O	K	M	O	A	S	A	N
N	R	F	R	R	E	E	Y	H	U	J	E	H	S	A	V	M	A	S	G	O	R	T	R	U
K	J	K	G	F	M	I	M	S	F	I	R	T	H	S	H	O	I	N	J	M	M	D	L	O
J	K	T	I	H	O	P	A	W	O	N	D	E	R	F	U	L	M	E	R	G	H	O	T	C
P	R	I	N	C	E	O	F	P	E	A	C	E	O	B	M	I	S	W	T	L	C	D	O	I

Bread of Life
Counselor
Emmanuel
Exemplar
First Born
Friend

Good Shepherd
Holy One
I am
Jehovah
Jesus Christ
King of Kings

Lamb of God
Light of the World
Lord
Master
Messiah
Only Begotten Son

Prince of Peace
Redeemer
Savior
Son of God
Wonderful

THESE THINGS WE DO

Word Scramble

• • • • • • • • • • • • • • • • •

Unscramble the words below to discover the things the Lord wants us to do to follow Him. Write each word on the lines in the scripture below.

1. LTAK
2. JROEICE
3. CEPAHR
4. OEPYSRHP
5. REWTI
6. DNECILHR
7. SRMINSOIE

"And we ______________ of Christ, we ______________ in Christ, we ______________ of Christ,
(1) (2) (3)

we ______________ of Christ and we ______________according to our prophecies, that our
(4) (5)

______________ may know to what source they may look for a ______________ of their sins"
(6) (7)

(2 Nephi 25:26).

Live Like His Son

Crossword

And then shall they know their Redeemer, who is Jesus Christ, the Son of God; and then shall they be gathered in from the four quarters of the earth unto their own lands, from whence they have been dispersed.

—3 Nephi 5:26

The scriptures teach us how to follow Jesus and what to do to live as He did. Use the scripture reference next to each clue if you need a hint.

Across

3. Ten given to Moses (2 Nephi 31:10)
5. To use your ears (D&C 100:2)
7. A talk with Heavenly Father (D&C 41:3)
8. Gifts from Heavenly Father (D&C 58:4)
9. To pay attention; listen (D&C 12:9)

Down

1 To keep the commandments (Deuteronomy 11:28)
2. Word of God (3 Nephi 23:14)
4. To help others (John 12:26)
6. Trust, belief (2 Timothy 3:15)
7. One who speaks for God (D&C 21:1)

Son of God

Hidden Message

Then spake Jesus again unto them, saying, I am the light of the world: he that followeth me shall not walk in darkness, but shall have the light of life.

—John 8:12

Cross off any word that has the letters **J, K, Q, X,** or **Z**. Read the remaining words from left to right for a message about whom we should follow on earth.

For	joy	unto	us	John	a	make
child	is	zoo	Jesus	born	quick	unto
just	join	us	a	keep	son	is
given	and	quiet	the	stake	government	shall
queen	journey	be	upon	his	exalt	shoulder
and	his	explain	name	key	shall	kind
excellent	Zion	be	called	extend	Wonderful	express
extra	Counselor	example	The	Mighty	take	God
The	quote	Everlasting	joyful	know	Father	kingdom
speak	The	Prince	of	Peace	know	text

(See Isaiah 9:6)

Let Him In

Maze

• • • • • • • • • • • • • • • • •

★Be	am	thy	given	Lord	love	prayer	by
day	father	thou	me	home	God	calling	do
God	all	pray	his	give	find	the	sent
that	humble	way	to	light	lead	still	walk
kind	parents	small	can	thy	live	earth	thee
and	has	child	and	dear	hand	has	beside
him	shall	care	with	he	help	answer	voice
here	must	and	of	the	me	teach	thee

Begin at the ★ and follow the instructions through the maze. Read the words in the blanks starting with number one to the end for an inspiring scripture about following Jesus.

1. ★_____________
2. Down 1 space, right 2 spaces _______________
3. Down 2 spaces, left 1 space _____________
4. 4 spaces down, 1 space right _______________
5. 2 spaces right ____________
6. 7 spaces up _______________
7. 2 spaces left ______________
8. 2 spaces down, 2 spaces left ______________
9. 4 spaces down, 1 space right ______________
10. 4 spaces right, 3 spaces up _______________
11. 4 spaces down, 2 spaces right _______________
12. 7 spaces up ______________
13. 2 spaces down, 1 space left ______________
14. 3 spaces down, 1 space left ________________
15. 2 spaces left______________
16. 3 spaces up, 1 space right __________________
17. 2 spaces down, 3 spaces right ______________
18. 2 spaces down, 1 space left ____________
19. 3 spaces left, 3 spaces up _____________
20. 1 space right, 1 space down _____________
21. 4 spaces up, 2 spaces right _____________

(See Doctrine and Covenants 112:10.)

What Would Jesus Do?

EZ Maze

They are free to choose liberty and
eternal life, through the great
Mediator of all men.
—2 Nephi 2:27

Trace the ★ symbol for a message about how you can follow Jesus.

★★★★★★★★★★★★★★ &&&&★★★★★★★★★★★★★★★★★&&&★★★★★★★★★★★★★★★★
★&&&&&&&&&&&&&&&&& ★ &&&&&&& ★&&&&&&&&&&★&
★&&&&&&&&&&&&&&&&& ★ &&&&&&& ★&&&&&&&&&&★&
★ &&&&&&&&&&&&&&&&&★ &&&&&&& ★&&&&&&&&&&★&
★&&&&&&&&&&&&&&&&& ★ &&&&&&& ★&&&&&&&&&&★&
★ &&&&&&&&&&&&&&&&&★ &&&&&&& ★★★★★★★★★★★★★★★★&
★&&&&&&&&&&&&&&&&& ★ &&&&&&& ★ &&&&&&&&&&
★&&&&&&&&&&&&&&&&& ★ &&&&&&& ★ & ★ &&&&&&&
★&&&&&&&&&&&&&&&&& ★ &&&&&&& & ★ && ★&&&&&&&
★ &&&&&&&&&&&&&&&&&★ &&&&&&& ★ &&& ★&&&&&&
★&&&&&&&&&&&&&&&&& ★ &&&&&&& &★ && &&& & ★ &&&
★★★★★★★★★★★★★★ &&&&&&& ★ &&&&&&& &★ &&&&&& & ★★★★

Be a Missionary

Word Search

And behold, I have been called to preach the word of God among all this people, according to the spirit of revelation and prophecy.

—Alma 8:24

Find the words that tell about missionaries in the word search below. A few can be found diagonally, as well as up and down and side to side.

O	B	E	D	I	E	N	T	P	P
U	R	A	I	E	L	D	E	R	S
A	G	F	P	Y	Y	D	A	E	C
U	O	O	U	T	L	R	C	A	R
T	S	P	I	R	I	T	H	C	I
H	P	H	O	E	A	Z	R	H	P
O	E	W	T	S	T	B	E	E	T
R	L	F	O	I	W	A	L	K	U
I	R	E	S	E	R	V	E	M	R
T	D	I	L	I	G	E	N	C	E
Y	V	E	F	A	M	I	L	Y	S
P	R	I	E	S	T	H	O	O	D

Authority	Obedient	Teach
Baptize	Preach	Visit
Diligence	Priesthood	Walk
Elders	Scriptures	World
Family	Serve	
Gospel	Spirit	

Be a Shepherd

Hidden Message

Ye will teach them to love one another,
and to serve one another.
—Mosiah 4:15

Color in each space that has a letter that rhymes with "tree," except e, d, and p. There will be one word in each row of letters. Read the words from left to right, top to bottom to find a special message.

G	F	T	E	Z	E	C	D	B
Z	C	B	M	T	G	Y	V	G
S	V	H	E	V	E	B	T	P

Missionary Songs

Matching

And if it so be that you should labor all your days in crying repentance unto this people, and bring, save it be one soul unto me, how great shall be your joy with him in the kingdom of my Father!

—Doctrine and Covenants 18:15

• • • • • • • • • • • • • • • • •

Match the title of a missionary song from the *Children's Songbook* with a phrase from that song. Write the letter next to the title and read the word from top to bottom that tells what missionaries are called to do.

_____ We'll Bring the World His Truth (p. 172)	C. Far and wide we tell the Father's story
_____ I Hope they Call Me on a Mission (p. 169)	M. To teach and preach the word of God
_____ I Want to be a Missionary Now (p. 168)	L. Receive the gospel light
_____ Called to Serve (p. 174)	P. We have been taught in our youth
_____ On a Golden Springtime (p. 88)	A. I'll follow him in faith
_____ The Church of Jesus Christ (p. 77)	O. I'll tell them how the gospel was restored
_____ The Fifth Article of Faith (p. 125)	I. To preach the gospel
_____ The Things I Do (p. 170)	R. I hope that I can share the gospel

MISSIONARY TALK

Scripture Find

• • • • • • • • • • • • • • • • •

Look up the scriptures and fill in the missing words. Write the underlined words in each scripture on the lines below to discover what missionaries say. Search out the final scripture when you're through.

1. "And blessed ________ (6) they who ________ (2) seek to bring forth my Zion at that day, for they shall have the gift and the power of the Holy ________ (12)" (1 Nephi 13:37).

2. "They had power and authority given unto them that they might _________ (3), and they also had what ________ (5) should speak given unto them" (Helaman 5:18).

3. "And it mattereth not unto me, if it so be that ________ (1) fill their mission, whether they go _______ (9) water or by land; let this be _____ (4) it is made known unto them according to their judgments hereafter" (Doctrine and Covenants 61:22).

4. "The testimony which ye have borne is recorded in heaven for _______ (10) angels to look ________ (8); and they rejoice over you, and your sins are forgiven you" (Doctrine and Covenants 62:3).

5. "Wherefore, stand ye in _______ (11) places, and be not ________ (7), until the day of the Lord come; for behold, it cometh quickly, saith the Lord" (Doctrine and Covenants 87:8).

"________ (1) __________ (2) __________ (3) _____ (4) _________ (5) _____ (6) __________ (7) ________ (8)

_____ (9) ______ (10) _______ (11) ___________ (12)" (Doctrine and Covenants 68:3).

Prepare to Be a Missionary

Logic

But purify your hearts before me; and then go ye into all the world, and preach my gospel unto every creature who has not received it.
—Doctrine and Covenants 112:28

When the Jones family (brothers Tom and James and sisters Ellie and Ruth) had a meeting, each child decided what they could learn to do to prepare for life as a missionary. From the clues below, see if you can find what each child learned to do. Cross out the names in the boxes according to the clues to reveal the answers.

1. Neither Ellie nor Tom was the child who polished everyone's Sunday shoes.
2. One of James's sisters studied the scriptures.
3. One of Ruth's brothers learned to iron shirts.
4. Tom was not the brother who made dinner and Ruth did not study the scriptures.

Ellie	James	Ruth	Tom	polished shoes
Ellie	James	Ruth	Tom	studied scriptures
Ellie	James	Ruth	Tom	ironed shirts
Ellie	James	Ruth	Tom	made dinner

WE SHARE TRUTH

Activity

Go ye therefore and teach all nations.
—Matthew 28:19–20

• • • • • • • • • • • • • • • • •

Match the symbol below each underlined space with the corresponding letter in the section below. Read the answer and discover what we can do to share truth.

& ♦   Δ Ω ♦   Δ #   * ♫ ♦   Δ Ω □ ¢   ▼ %

_ _ _ _ _ _ _. _ _   _ _ _ _   _ _ _ _   _ _ _ _ _ _

♫ ♦ ► Δ □ Δ ☼   & ♦   ♫ Δ ^ ♦   ☻ ♦ ♦ ☼   * Δ ¶ ♣ ♫ *

_ _   _ _ _   _ _ _ _ _.   _ _ _   _ _   _ _ _ _   _ _

☺ ☼   ▼ ¶ Ω   ¢ ▼ ¶ * ♫   Δ ☼ ♥   & ♦   & ☺ ► ►   ☻ ♦

_ _ _   _ _ _ _ _'_   _ _ _ _ _ _ _ _ _ _ _ _   _ _

* ♫ ♦   ► ▼ Ω ♥ #   □ ☺ # # ☺ ▼ ☼ Δ Ω ☺ ♦ #   * ▼

_ _ _ _ _   _ _ _   _ _ _ _ _   _ _ _   _ _ _ _ _.

☻ Ω ☺ ☼ ♣   * ♫ ♦   & ▼ Ω ► ♥   ♫ ☺ #   * Ω ¶ * ♫

A= Δ	G=♣	N=☼	U=¶
B =☻	H=♫	O=▼	V=^
D=♥	I=☺	R= Ω	W=&
E=♦	L=►	S=#	Y=¢

("We'll Bring the World His Truth," *Children's Songbook*, 172–173)

What Do We Teach?

Missing Letter Words

I will make an instrument of thee in my hands unto the salvation of many souls.
—Alma 17:11

• • • • • • • • • • • • • • • • •

Every other letter is missing from the phrases below. The letters are listed in alphabetical order in the box beside each phrase. Replace each letter to find words that tell what missionaries are to do. The scripture reference will help if you get stuck. When you finish, put the highlighted letters (in order) on the lines below to spell out what missionaries are to teach.

1. prepared thee for a g __ e __ t __ r ▬ o __ k (Doctrine and Covenants 39:11)	a e r r w
2. t __ e __ d __ d ▬ b __ y (Alma 57:21)	e h i o y
3. p __ e __ c __ ▬ e __ e __ t __ n __ e (Doctrine and Covenants 44:3)	a a c h n p r r
4. t __ a __ h __ e __ o ▬ o t __ y __ i __ l (Psalms 143:10)	c d e h l m t w
5. ▬ p __ n __ o __ r __ o __ t __ (Doctrine and Covenants 30:11)	e h m o u u y
6. b __ p __ i __ i __ g in the name o __ t __ e ▬ a __ h __ r (Doctrine and Covenants 68:8)	a e f f h n t t z
7. __ r __ a __ h __ y ▬ o __ p __ l (Doctrine and Covenants 112:28)	c e e g m p s
8. administer i __ t __ e ▬ r __ i __ a __ c __ s (Articles of Faith 1:5)	e d h n n n o
9. serve God __ i __ h __ l __ ▬ i __ i __ e __ c __ (3 Nephi 5:3)	a d e g l l n t w

___ ___ ___ ___   ___ ___   ___ ___ ___

I'll Go Where You Want Me to Go

EZ Maze

In the midst of heaven, having the everlasting gospel to preach unto them that dwell on the earth, and to every nation, and kindred, and tongue, and people.
—Revelation 14:6

Trace the lines next to the missionary nametags to see the way the missionary will travel to get to his mission.

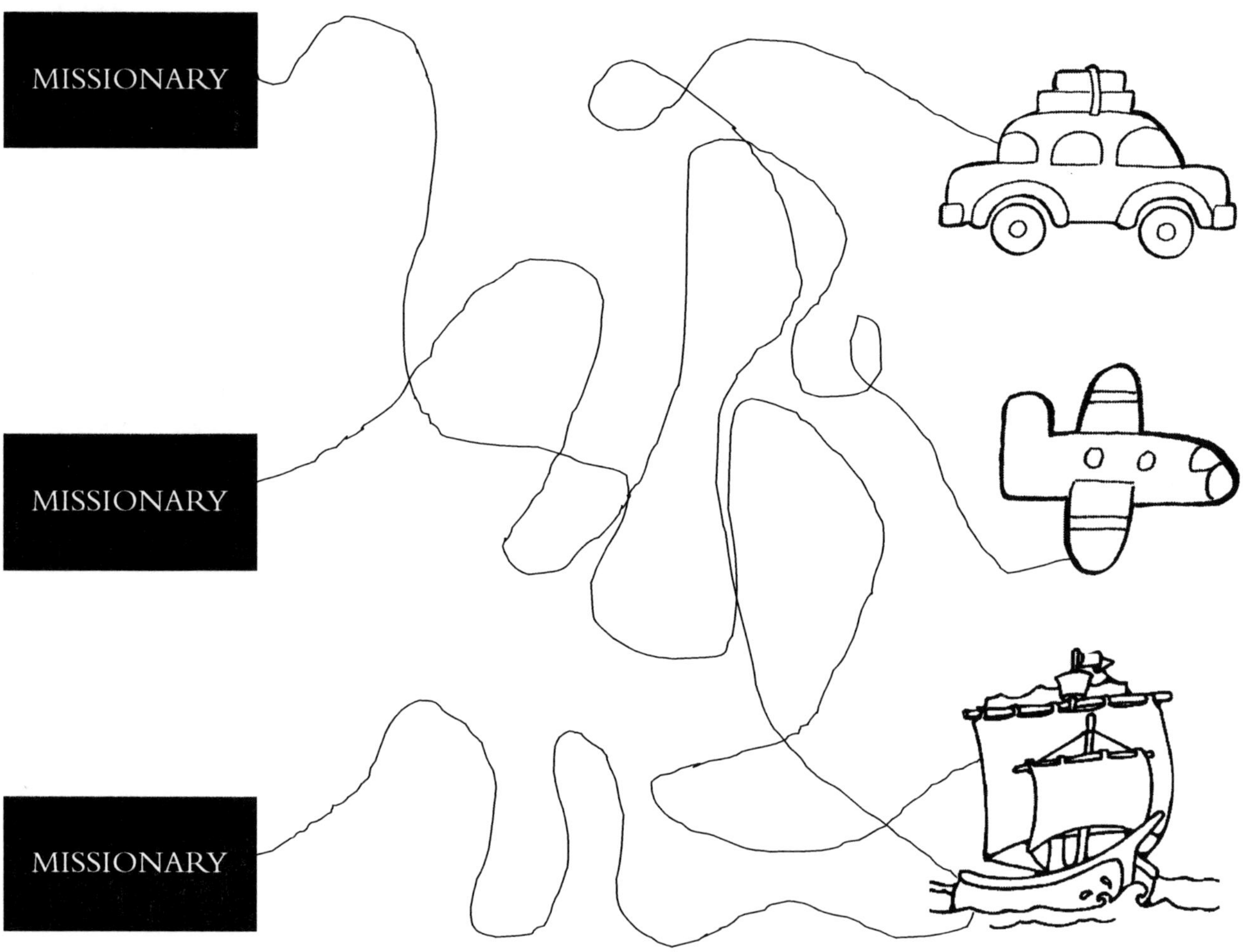

Heavenly Servants

Word Scramble

• • • • • • • • • • • • • • • • •

Unscramble the following words below and place the word in the scripture. Use the clue beside the scrambled word to help you.

1. isthng—a bunch of stuff
2. misdow—we have this when we are wise
3. rlena—what we do when someone teaches us
4. lofelw—a person you know
5. cevsrie—doing something for someone else

"And behold I tell you these ________________ (1) that ye may learn ________________ (2); that ye may ________________ (3) that when ye are in the service of your ________________ (4) beings ye are only in the ________________ (5) of your God" (Mosiah 2:17).

Preach the Word

Crossword

It is my will that you should proclaim my gospel from land to land, and from city to city, yea, in those regions round about where it has not been proclaimed.
—Doctrine and Covenants 66:5

The scriptures teach us about missionaries and what they should do. Use the scripture reference next to each clue if you need a hint.

Across

2. Move your feet (2 Corinthians 5:7)
3. To say what you believe (John 15:26)
6. A talk with Heavenly Father (D&C 42:14)
8. To instruct (2 Nephi 12:3)
9. To give of yourself (D&C 4:2)

Down

1. To become a member of the Church (Matthew 3:11)
2. Baptism clothing color (Mormon 9:6)
4. The Word of God (John 5:39)
5. The Holy Ghost is a ___ (John 1:33).
7. Good news (D&C 50:14)

Crossing the Plains

Crossword

Let all the people of the Church of Jesus Christ of Latter-day Saints, and those who journey with them, be organized into companies, with a covenant and promise to keep all the commandments and statutes of the Lord our God.

—Doctrine and Covenants 136:2

Pioneers had many challenges when they crossed the plains. Find some of those challenges listed in this puzzle. When you have solved the puzzle, unscramble the highlighted letters to discover something important to the pioneers.

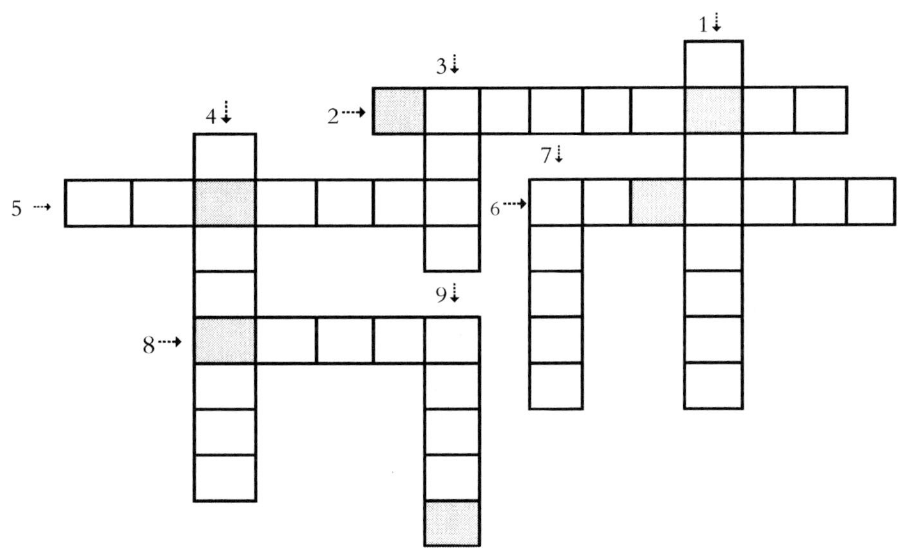

___ ___ ___ ___ ___ ___

Clues

1. Opposite of health
2. Tall, rock structures
3. Animals used to pull a wagon
4. Where the pioneers would gather at night
5. Plains or meadows
6. Using your feet to get somewhere
7. Used to carry things across the plains
8. Trust in the Lord
9. Opposite of sad

Pioneer Handcarts

Matching

And this shall be our covenant—that we will walk in all the ordinances of the Lord.
—Doctrine and Covenants 136:4

Match each word below with the meaning of that word. Then put the letter from the match on the blanks below (according to the matched number) to spell out where the handcart pioneers were going.

1. Family	L. To move by dragging
2. Pioneers	A. Those who came to Utah in wagons or handcarts
3. Pulling	Y. The round parts of handcarts
4. Pushing	V. Parents, children, and grandparents
5. Walking	L. To move by leaning on
6. Wheels	E. Using your feet to move

___ ___ ___ ___ ___ ___
1 2 3 4 5 6

Wagon Gear

Word Scramble

Organize yourselves; prepare every needful thing.
—Doctrine and Covenants 88:119

Unscramble the answer word for the clue for an item that you might find on a wagon crossing the plains.

1. Used for healing the sick:
   i m e n i d c e
2. Two- or four-legged creatures such as oinkers, mooers, and cluckers:
   l i a m s n a
3. Used to see at night:
   a n l t n r e
4. Containers used to cook food over a hot campfire:
   t e s e l k t
5. Coverings to keep warm on cold nights:
   n b l e s a k t
6. Shelter to sleep inside:
   e t n t
7. Used for hunting:
   o b w d n a r w r a o
8. Used for building, plowing, and repairing things:
   l o t o s
9. Small items used to grow plants:
   e e s s d
10. Books that contain the gospel:
    p r s u s r c e i t
11. Covering for the body:
    n c o g i t h l
12. Used for washing clothing:
    d w s r b a o a h

Westward Trek

Logic

And behold, I tell you these things that ye may learn wisdom; that ye may learn that when ye are in the service of your fellow beings ye are only in the service of your God.

—Mosiah 2:17

The girls in the Davies family were each assigned an item to be responsible for on the trek west. From the clues given, can you figure out which girl has which responsibility?

1. Neither Emily nor Lizzie is taking care of the lantern.
2. Neither of the girls whose name begins with the letter M is taking care of the food or the lantern.
3. Either Emily or Mandy will take care of the clothing.
4. Lizzie and Missy are not taking care of the kettle, but one of them will take care of the blanket.
5. Neither Emily nor Lizzie will take care of the clothing.

Family Member			**Responsibility**		
Emily	lantern	blanket	clothing	kettle	food
Mandy	lantern	blanket	clothing	kettle	food
Sarah	lantern	blanket	clothing	kettle	food
Missy	lantern	blanket	clothing	kettle	food
Lizzie	lantern	blanket	clothing	kettle	food

Pioneers Today

Letter Clue

And let my servants that have been appointed go and teach this, my will, to the saints, that they may be ready to go to a land of peace.
—Doctrine and Covenants 136:16

Write the word for each definition. Then write the numbered letters below to complete a line from a song in the *Children's Songbook* about how we can be pioneers today. Look it up when you're through.

1. The opposite of east ___ ___ ___ ___ (1, 23, 13)
2. A pioneer vehicle pulled by people ___ ___ ___ ___ ___ ___ ___ ___ (22, 29, 16, 20)
3. To move by car, boat or plane ___ ___ ___ ___ ___ ___ (10, 2, 30)
4. Low land between hills or mountains ___ ___ ___ ___ ___ ___ (25, 12, 32, 17)
5. Blowing air ___ ___ ___ ___ (33, 5, 27)
6. Larger than a hill ___ ___ ___ ___ ___ ___ ___ ___ (9, 6, 24, 19)
7. Round parts on a pioneer wagon ___ ___ ___ ___ ___ ___ (18, 26, 3)
8. What we do in church on Sunday ___ ___ ___ ___ ___ ___ ___ (15, 8, 21, 31, 11)
9. Walking up and down hills ___ ___ ___ ___ ___ ___ (14, 28, 4, 7)

"___ ___
1 2 3 4 5 6 7 8 9 10 11 12 13 14 15 16 17 18 19 20 21

___ ___ ___ ___ ___ ___ ___ ___ ___ ___ ___ ___" (*Children's Songbook*, 215)
22 23 24 25 26 27 28 29 30 31 32 33

Searching for Zion

Word Search

And it shall come to pass, when ye be come to the land which the Lord will give you, according as he hath promised, that ye shall keep this service.
—Exodus 12:25

Search in all directions for the words that tell some of the things associated with the pioneers while traveling to search for Zion.

W	G	A	M	F	J	O	X	E	N	G	C
A	N	C	H	H	D	P	G	S	N	F	A
L	I	E	A	L	P	L	A	I	N	S	E
K	T	D	N	M	C	R	G	V	O	U	D
I	N	F	D	B	P	N	E	S	T	P	R
N	A	L	C	J	I	F	A	O	R	P	A
G	L	G	A	S	E	A	I	M	K	L	W
D	P	K	R	O	H	M	F	R	B	I	T
F	A	I	T	H	P	I	D	H	E	E	S
B	E	M	C	K	B	L	C	P	L	S	E
C	A	H	P	R	A	Y	I	N	G	D	W
I	L	L	N	E	S	S	G	R	F	J	B

Campfire
Faith
Family
Handcart
Illness
Oxen
Plains
Planting
Praying
Singing
Supplies
Walking
Westward

Westward Ho!

EZ Dot

And he said, Let us take our journey,
and let us go, and I will go before thee.
—Genesis 33:12

Begin at the star and trace the outside circle. Begin at each heart and draw a line from the heart to the center circle to complete the picture.

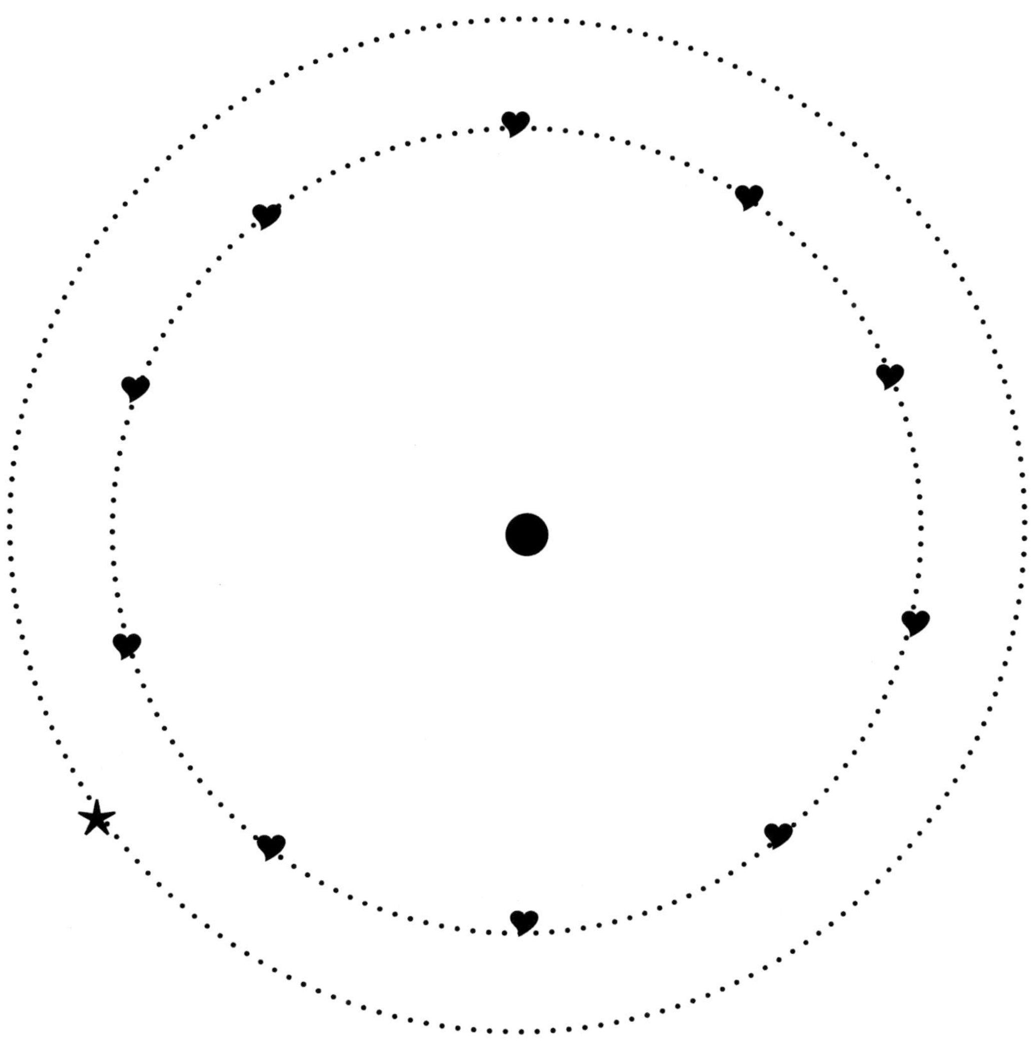

O, PIONEERS!

Missing Letter Words

Let each company provide themselves with all the
teams, wagons, provisions, clothing, and other
necessaries for the journey, that they can.
—Doctrine and Covenants 136:5

• •

Every other letter is missing from the phrases below. The letters are listed in alphabetical order in the box beside the phrase. Replace each letter to find phrases that tell about how the pioneers were to prepare for their journey. The scripture references have the answers if you get stuck.

1. p __ t __ i __ g   __ n   __ p __ i __ g   __ r __ p __
   (Doctrine and Covenants 136:7)

c i o n n r s s t u

2. __ o __ e __ a __ t   __ n __   p __ o __ i __ e
   (Doctrine and Covenants 136:2)

a c d m n n r s v

3. t __ a __ s,   __ a __ o __ s,   __ r __ v __ s __ o __ s,
   __ l __ t __ i __ g (Doctrine and Covenants 136:5)

c e g h i i m n n n o o p w

4. __ i __ h   __   p __ r __   h __ a __ t
   (Doctrine and Covenants 136:11)

a e e r t u w

5. __ r __ i __ e   __ h __   L __ r __   w __ t __
   s __ n __ i __ g (Doctrine and Covenants 136:28)

a d e g h i i n o p s t

6. r __ a __ y   __ o   __ o   __ o   __   l __ n __   o __
   p __ a __ e (Doctrine and Covenants 136:16)

a a c d d e e f g t t

7. p __ e __ a __ e   __ o __   t __ o __ e   __ h __   a __ e
   __ o   __ a __ r __ (Doctrine and Covenants 136:6)

f h o p r r r r r s t t w y

Pioneer Journeys

Scripture Find

• • • • • • • • • • • • • • • • •

Each scripture below has a missing word. Choose the right word and read the clue. Put the correct letter on the lines below to make a word that tells of something the pioneers made before they left on their journey.

1. "And from this place ye shall go forth into the regions ________; and inasmuch as ye shall find them that will receive you ye shall build up my church in every region" (Doctrine and Covenants 42:8).
   If the word is around, *write the letter* **I**. *If it is* westward, *write the letter* **C**.

2. "Let each company provide themselves with all the teams, _________, provisions, clothing, and other necessaries for the journey, that they can" (Doctrine and Covenants 136:5).
   If the word is wagons, *write the letter* **O**. *If it is* shelters, *write the letter* **M**.

3. "Let each company, with their captains and presidents, decide how many can go next spring; then choose out a sufficient number of able–bodied and expert men, . . . to go as ________ to prepare for putting in spring crops" (Doctrine and Covenants 136:7).
   If the word is farmers, *write the letter* **M**. *If it is* pioneers, *write the letter* **V**.

4. "And if ye do this with a pure heart, in all ___________, ye shall be blessed; you shall be blessed in your flocks, and in your herds, and in your fields, and in your houses, and in your families" (Doctrine and Covenants 136:11).
   If the word is honesty, *write the letter* **A**. *If it is* faithfulness, *write the letter* **E**.

5. "If thou art merry, praise the Lord with singing, with music, with _________, and with a prayer of praise and thanksgiving" (Doctrine and Covenants 136:28).
   If the word is dancing, *write the letter* **N**. *If it is* rejoicing, *write the letter* **R**.

6. "Be strong and of a good _________, fear not, nor be afraid of them: for the LORD thy God, he *it is* that doth go with thee; he will not fail thee, nor forsake thee" (Deuteronomy 31:6).
   If the word is courage, *write the letter* **A**. *If it is* faith, *write the letter* **C**.

7. "Six days shall work be done: but the seventh day *is* the sabbath of_______, an holy convocation; ye shall do no work *therein:* it *is* the sabbath of the LORD in all your dwellings" (Leviticus 23:3).
   If the word is God, *write the letter* **E**. *If it is* rest, *write the letter* **N**.

8. "And all saints who remember to keep and do these sayings, _________ in obedience to the commandments, shall receive health in their navel and marrow to their bones" (Doctrine and Covenants 89:18).
   If the word is walking, *write the letter* **T**. *If it is* being, *write the letter* **P**.

___ ___ ___ ___ ___ ___ ___ ___ (see Doctrine and Covenants 136:4).
1 2 3 4 5 6 7 8

Gospel Truth

Hidden Message

And the gospel of Jesus Christ shall be
declared among them.
—2 Nephi 30:5

• • • • • • • • • • • • • • • • •

Draw a line from letter to letter in a zigzag pattern starting with the first letter on the bottom line, and then going up to the second letter on the top line. Place each letter in the zig zag pattern on the line below to reveal a message about a special time. Next, circle every other letter on the bottom line, beginning with the second letter. Place the letters on the line below the first message to reveal a great prophet.

J H R G E S T E K R M S E O F E V T U T L E T A E T I

T J E O O S P E L P E H T S R M D I O T H H E J R R H

__ __ __   __ __ __ __ __ __   __ __ __ __ __ __ __ __   __ __

__ __ __   __ __ __ __ __.

__ __ __ __ __ __   __ __ __ __ __   __ __.

Hallowed Ground

Hidden Message

Let us take our journey, and let us go,
and I will go before thee.
—Genesis 33:12

Circle every other letter to reveal the name of the prophet who helped the Saints to cross the plains to the Salt Lake Valley. Start with the fifth letter, which is in **bold**, and end with the fifth-to-last-letter, which is in **bold**. Then write down the letters remaining to reveal what this leader said when he arrived in the Salt Lake Vally.

T H I S **B** I R S I T G H H E A R M I Y G O H U T N P **G** L A C E

__ __ __ __   __ __   __ __ __   __ __ __ __ __.

He Said It! He Did It!

Matching

That he may prophesy concerning
all things.
—Moroni 10:13

Match the clue in the left column with the corresponding prophet in the right column. Place the letter at the beginning of the clue answer on the line below with the corresponding number to tell something that prophets reveal.

1. Mormon	R. Parted the Red Sea for the Israelites
2. Moses	S. Crossed the plains with the Saints
3. Gordon B. Hinckley	P. Hid the sacred records in the Hill Cumorah
4. Joseph Smith	E. Interpreted dreams for Pharaoh
5. Nephi	O. Gave us six be's to follow
6. Joseph of Egypt	H. Stated he was born of goodly parents
7. Brigham Young	P. Prayed to God in a wooded grove of trees
8. Daniel	S. Said to "Read the Book of Mormon"
9. Jesus Christ	I. Tamed the lions in a den
10. Ezra Taft Benson	E. Said, "This is my commandment I say unto you, love one another as I have loved you."

___ ___ ___ ___ ___ ___ ___ ___ ___ ___
1 2 3 4 5 6 7 8 9 10

Heavenly Father's Voice on Earth

Code

We believe in the same organization
that existed in the primitive church,
namely, apostles, prophets . . .
—Articles of Faith 1:6

• • • • • • • • • • • • • • • • •

Using the phrases below, add or subtract parts of the words given to come up with a new letter or word. Print the new letter or word on the line. Read the answers in order from top to bottom for a special message.

Went – nt = ___________

Things – ings + ank = ____________

Theater – ater + e = _____________

The letter between n and p = _____________

Go + d = ______________

Fortune – tune = ________________

The first letter of the alphabet = ___________

Pro + phone – one + et = _____________

(*Hymns*, no. 19)

Old Testament Prophets Teach

Scripture Find

• • • • • • • • • • • • • • • • •

Each scripture below has a missing word. Find the word, read the clue, and put the correct word on the lines below to complete a scripture about prophets.

1. "And they went in unto Noah into the ______, two and two of all flesh, wherein is the breath of life" (Genesis 7:15).
   If the missing word is ship, *write* **the**. *If it is* ark, *write* **revealeth**.
2. "Seeing that Abraham shall surely become a great and mighty _________, and all the nations of the earth shall be blessed in him" (Genesis 18:18).
   If the missing word is nation, *write* **his**. *If it is* people, *write* **prophet**.
3. "And Moses stretched out his hand over the sea; and the LORD caused the sea to go back by a strong east wind all that night, and made the sea dry land, and the waters were _________" (Exodus 14:21).
   If the missing word is divided, *write* **secret**. *If it is* parted, *write* **therefore**.
4. "And Enoch and all his people __________ with God, and he dwelt in the midst of Zion; and it came to pass that Zion was not, for God received it up into his own bosom; and from thence went forth the saying, ZION IS FLED" (Moses 7:69).
   If the missing word is talked, *write* **thus**. *If it is* walked, *write* **unto**.
5. "And now, behold, I say unto you, that ye ought to search these things. Yea, a commandment I give unto you that ye search these things diligently; for great are the _________ of Isaiah" (3 Nephi 23:1).
   If the missing word is words, *write* **his**. *If it is* teachings, *write* **gospel**.
6. "And also Elijah, unto whom I have committed the _________of the power of turning the hearts of the fathers to the children, and the hearts of the children to the fathers, that the whole earth may not be smitten with a curse" (D&C 27:9).
   If the missing word is blessing, *write* **of**. *If it is* keys, *write* **servants**.
7. "So Jeremiah wrote in a ___________all the evil that should come upon Babylon, even all these words that are written against Babylon" (Jeremiah 51:60).
   If the missing word is book, *write* **the**. *If it is* cave, *write* **thy**.
8. "Now the Lord had prepared a great fish to ____________up Jonah. And Jonah was in the belly of the fish three days and three nights" (Jonah 1:17).
   If the missing word is lift, *write* **Lord**. *If it is* swallow, *write* **prophets**.

"Surely the Lord God will do nothing, but he _____________ (1) _____ (2) ___________ (3)

______ (4) _____ (5) _____________ (6) _____ (7) ________________ (8)" (Amos 3:7).

Organized Like Times of Old

Word Scramble

• • • • • • • • • • • • • • • • •

Unscramble the words below to discover the titles of leaders in our church. Put each unscrambled word on the numbered line in the scripture below.

1. sasepolt
2. esphorpt
3. srpatos
4. hceetras
5. seaivgtnels

"We believe in the first organization that existed in the primitive church, namely,

____________, ____________, ____________, ____________, ____________, and so forth"
1 2 3 4 5

(Articles of Faith 1:6).

Power on Earth

Hidden Message

For there is not a place found on earth that he may come to and restore again that which was lost unto you, or which he hath taken away, even the fulness of the priesthood.

—Doctrine and Covenants 124:28

Color in all the words that contain the letters: B, C, F, or Y.
Read the remaining words from left to right for a message about power on earth.

joy	The	young	birth	priesthood	search	is	forever	calm	came
restored,	youth	church	the	baptized	change	hymn	fast	truth	tarry
pray	made	known	care	scripture	to	try	man,	can	That
God	yearn	clean	has	spoken	may	to	brother	the	be
happy	earth,	you	blessing	belong	his	family	power	believe	is
father	life	here	choice	boy	again.	child	receive	holy	baby

("The Priesthood Is Restored," *Children's Songbook*, 89)

Six Be's to Follow

Crossword

Behold, they are they which shall
not perish.
—2 Nephi 26:8

Across

2. Using your mind well
3. Opposite of dirty
5. Full of prayer
6. Rhymes with bumble; meek

Down

1. To be thankful
4. Trumpet – mpt (subtract the letters m, p, and t)

WHAT A PROPHET DOES

Code

Behold, here is wisdom; yea, to be a seer, a revelator,
a translator, and a prophet, having all the gifts of God
which he bestows upon the head of the church.
—Doctrine and Covenants 107:92

Using the code grid below, find the words listed by matching the shape with the letter in it. Write the letters in each clue shape. Complete the list of words and discuss with someone how each word is related to the prophets.

A	D	E
L	O	R
S	T	U

1.  C H
2. 
3. G  I 
4. F 
5.  V 
6. 
7.  P  K

Which Prophet Said That?

Logic

I will raise them up a Prophet from among their brethren, like unto thee, and will put my words in his mouth; and he shall speak unto them all that I shall command him.

—Deuteronomy 18:18

• •

Can you find out which prophet was known for which saying? Use the grid below to help you. Put an X in each box if it cannot be true and a circle if it is true. Don't forget that one of them is remembered for saying, "Come to the temple."

1. Neither David O. McKay nor Gordon B. Hinckley is remembered for saying, "Lengthen your stride."
2. "Read the Book of Mormon" was the counsel of a prophet without an "L" in his name.
3. Ezra Taft Benson became the prophet right after Spencer W. Kimball.
4. Gordon B. Hinckley was not the one remembered for saying, "Every member a missionary."
5. David O. McKay was not known for saying, "Read the Book of Mormon."

	"Come to the Temple"	"Every Member a Missionary"	"Lengthen Your Stride"	"Read the Book of Mormon"
David O. McKay				
Ezra Taft Benson				
Gordon B. Hinckley				
Spencer W. Kimball				

Follow His Words

EZ Maze

Hear ye the words of the prophet.
—1 Nephi 19:24

President Hinckley's "Be's" will help you through this maze and can guide you in the choices you make in life.

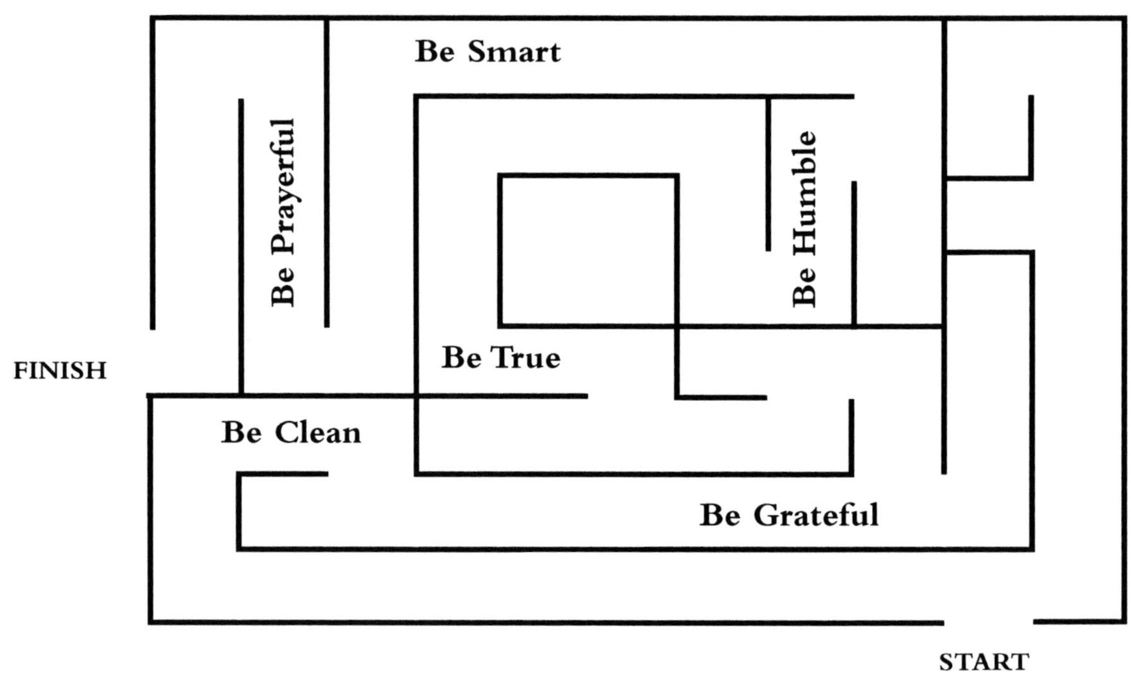

AT CHURCH

Matching

And that thou mayest more fully keep thyself unspotted
from the world, thou shalt go to the house of prayer
and offer up thy sacraments upon my holy day.
—Doctrine and Covenants 59:9

Match each word below with the meaning of that word. Then put the letter from the match on the blanks below (according to the matched number) to spell out something we do at church.

1. Sacrament	I. The leader of the ward
2. Prayer	H. Those who teach children the gospel
3. Primary	O. "We thank thee"
4. Singing	P. To give heed to what the prophet says
5. Teachers	R. Where children learn the gospel
6. Bishop	S. "I Am a Child of God"
7. Listen	W. Bread and water taken each week

___ ___ ___ ___ ___ ___ ___
1 2 3 4 5 6 7

Blessed Be the Day

Hidden Message

And they shall also teach their children
to pray, and to walk uprightly before
the Lord.
—Doctrine and Covenants 68:28

Color in all the words that tell what you can do on the Sabbath day. Hint: the words will end in *-ing*. Read the remaining words to reveal a scripture about the Sabbath day. Look up the scripture when you are through.

praying	and	reading	singing	the	writing	resting	inhabitants	visiting	fasting
of	Zion	driving	studying	pondering	shall	listening	obeying	also	journaling
thinking	repenting	observe	honoring	meeting	sleeping	the	Sabbath	teaching	coloring
day	eating	painting	to	learning	keep	educating	serving	it	holy

(Doctrine and Covenants 68:29)

Day of Rest

Code

Six days may work be done; but in the seventh is the sabbath of rest.
—Exodus 31:15

• • • • • • • • • • • • • • • • •

Under each letter below, place the letter that follows it in the alphabet. Continue through to the end and see an important message. For the letter Z, use the letter A.

Q D L D L A D Q   S G D   R Z A A Z S G   C Z X

_ _ _ _ _ _ _ _   _ _ _   _ _ _ _ _ _ _   _ _ _

S N   J D D O   H S   G N K X

_ _   _ _ _ _   _ _   _ _ _ _.

(Exodus 20:8)

Modern Day Plates

Word Search

I beheld other books which came forth
by the power of the Lamb.
—1 Nephi 13:39

Search in all directions for the names of the books in the Book of Mormon.

2	R	H	P	E	M	O	R	M	O	N	T	E	I
N	T	J	A	R	O	M	L	J	M	V	R	N	H
E	H	P	E	S	K	A	E	J	A	C	O	B	S
P	V	T	1	N	E	P	H	I	K	R	P	T	M
H	M	S	K	J	R	X	M	W	O	R	O	H	E
I	W	O	R	D	S	O	F	M	O	R	M	O	N
H	L	A	S	X	V	K	I	H	P	E	N	3	O
E	P	M	M	I	H	P	E	N	4	L	I	P	S
H	E	L	A	M	A	N	P	H	T	P	S	M	P
R	M	A	S	E	T	H	R	J	E	T	H	E	R

1 Nephi	Jarom	Mosiah	4 Nephi
2 Nephi	Omni	Alma	Mormon
Jacob	Words of	Helaman	Ether
Enos	Mormon	3 Nephi	Moroni

Sabbath Day Choices

Letter Clue

Write the answer to the clue about things we do on the Sabbath day. Place the numbered letters below to complete the scripture about the Sabbath day. Look the scripture up when you are through.

1. On Sundays we go to ___ ___ ___ ___ ___ ___
   7 13 31

2. We read the ___ ___ ___ ___ ___ ___ ___ ___ ___ ___
   1 19 6 37 2 25

3. Uses symbols of bread and water ___ ___ ___ ___ ___ ___ ___ ___ ___
   33 4 29 22

4. Another word for hymns ___ ___ ___ ___ ___
   36 5 8

5. Where we meet for sharing time ___ ___ ___ ___ ___ ___ ___
   39 16 34

6. Families can be together ___ ___ ___ ___ ___ ___ ___
   9 18 3 20

7. Go to see someone ___ ___ ___ ___ ___
   27 21 30

8. Search, ___ ___ ___ ___ ___ ___ , and pray
   12 10 26

9. To concentrate on something deeply ___ ___ ___ ___ ___ ___ ___ ___
   15 23 17 40 42

10. Lord's code of health we follow ___ ___ ___ ___ ___ ___ ___ ___ ___ ___ ___ ___
    11 24 35 41

11. ___ ___ ___ ___ the Sabbath ___ ___ ___ holy.
    14 28 32

12. We study the ___ ___ ___ ___ of Mormon and Bible.
    38

"And on the ___ ___ ___ ___ ___ ___ ___ day ___ ___ ___ ended his ___ ___ ___ ___ which he had
1 2 3 4 5 6 7 8 9 10 11 12 13 14

___ ___ ___ ___ ; and he ___ ___ ___ ___ ___ ___ on the ___ ___ ___ ___ ___ ___ ___ ___ ___ ___ from
15 16 17 18 19 20 21 22 23 24 25 26 27 28 29 30 31 32 33 34

all his ___ ___ ___ ___ which he had ___ ___ ___ ___" (Genesis 2:2).
35 36 37 38 39 40 41 42

SABBATH DAY GIFT

Scripture Find

• • • • • • • • • • • • • • • • •

Each scripture below has a missing word. Choose the right word and read the clue. Put the correct letter on the lines below to make a word that tells of something we partake of on the Sabbath day.

1. "Remember the sabbath day, to keep it ________" (Exodus 20:8).
   If the word is holy, *write the letter* **S**. *If it is* hallowed, *write the letter* **C**.

2. "Ye shall keep my sabbaths, and __________ my sanctuary: I am the LORD" (Leviticus 19:30).
   If the word is reverence, *write the letter* **A**. *If it is* enter, *write the letter* **H**.

3. "O come, let us _________ and bow down: let us kneel before the LORD our maker" (Psalms 95:6).
   If the word is pray, *write the letter* **M**. *If it is* worship, *write the letter* **C**.

4. After this manner therefore pray ye: Our Father which art in heaven, __________ be thy name" (Matthew 6:9).
   If the word is blessed, *write the letter* **A**. *If it is* hallowed, *write the letter* **R**.

5. "Let the word of Christ dwell in you richly in all wisdom; teaching and admonishing one another in psalms and _________ and spiritual songs, singing with grace in your hearts to the Lord" (Colossians 3:16).
   If the word is hymns, *write the letter* **A**. *If it is* scriptures, *write the letter* **L**.

6. "____________ to the words of Christ, your Redeemer, your Lord and your God" (Moroni 8:8).
   If the word is obedient, *write the letter* **I**. *If it is* listen, *write the letter* **M**.

7. "Six days may work be done; but in the seventh is the sabbath of ______, holy to the Lord" (Exodus 31:15).
   If the word is God, *write the letter* **G**. *If it is* rest, *write the letter* **E**.

8. "And he who receiveth all things with _____________ shall be made glorious; and the things of this earth shall be added unto him, even an hundred fold, yea, more" (Doctrine and Covenants 78:19).
   If the word is thankfulness, *write the letter* **N**. *If it is gratitude, write the letter* **O**.

9. "And that this house may be a house of ________, a house of fasting, a house of faith, a house of glory and of God, even thy house" (Doctrine and Covenants 109.16).
   If the word is prayer, *write the letter* **T**. *If it is* learning, *write the letter* **R**.

_____	_____	_____	_____	_____	_____	_____	_____	_____
1	2	3	4	5	6	7	8	9

(See D&C 27:2)

The Way to Church

EZ Maze

Thou shalt go to the house of prayer and offer up thy sacraments upon my holy day.

—Doctrine and Covenants 59:9

Can you help the children find the way to church?

TRUE WORSHIP

Code

And he commanded them that they should observe
the sabbath day, and keep it holy, and also every day
they should give thanks to the Lord their God.
—Mosiah 18:23

• •

Discover the counting pattern in the code below. Use the code to fill in the words of the scripture. A letter has the same number throughout the quotation. This scripture tells us how we should worship Heavenly Father on the Sabbath day. Search out the scripture when you're through.

___	___	9	12	___	___	___
A	B	C	D	E	G	H

___	___	30	___	___	___	___
I	L	M	N	O	P	R

___	___	___	___	___	60
S	T	U	V	W	Y

"Take upon you the name of Christ, and

___ ___ ___ ___ ___ ___ ___   ___ ___ ___,   ___ ___
57 36 42 45 21 24 39   18 36 12   24 33

___ ___ ___ ___ ___ ___ ___ ___ ___ ___   ___ ___ ___ ___ ___
57 21 3 48 45 36 15 54 15 42   39 27 3 9 15

___ ___   ___ ___ ___   ___ ___   ___ ___,   ___ ___
60 15   30 3 60   6 15   24 33   24 33

___ ___ ___ ___ ___ ___   ___ ___ ___   ___ ___   ___ ___ ___ ___ ___"
45 39 24 42 24 48   3 33 12   24 33   48 42 51 48 21

(Alma 34:38).

What Do You Do on the Sabbath?

Missing Letter Words

Then said Jesus unto them, I will ask
you one thing; Is it lawful on the
sabbath days to do good?
—Luke 6:9

Every other letter is missing from the words below. The letters are listed in alphabetical order in the box beside the phrase. Replace each letter to find words that tell what you do on the Sabbath day.

1. __ t __ e __ d __ h __ r __ h	a c c n t u
2. r __ a __ s __ r __ p __ u __ e __	c d e i r s t
3. s __ t __ e __ e __ e __ t __ y	i l n r r v
4. __ a __ t __ n __ p __ a __	a d f r s y
5. v __ s __ t __ t __ e __ s	i i h o r
6. __ a __ i __ y __ c __ i __ i __ i __ s	a e f l m t t v

When We Go to Church

Letter Clue

Holding fast the faithful word as he
hath been taught.

—Titus 1:9

• • • • • • • • • • • • • • • • •

Write the word for each definition. Then write the numbered letters below to complete a scripture about the importance of the Sabbath day. Look it up when you're through.

1. Father, mother, and children ___ ___ ___ ___ ___ ___ (26, 9, 28, 17)
2. Bread and water ___ ___ ___ ___ ___ ___ ___ ___ ___ (8, 23, 16, 3, 22, 5)
3. Church room with pews ___ ___ ___ ___ ___ ___ (6, 12, 2)
4. Keep the commandments to be ___ ___ ___ ___ ___ ___ ___ ___ (10, 15, 25, 29)
5. A talk with Heavenly Father ___ ___ ___ ___ ___ ___ (4, 27, 7)
6. To speak ___ ___ ___ ___ (13, 21, 1)
7. One tenth; given to the Church ___ ___ ___ ___ ___ ___ ___ (18, 24, 14)
8. The father of our ward ___ ___ ___ ___ ___ ___ (11, 20, 19)

"___ ___ ___ ___   ___ ___ ___   ___ ___ ___ ___ ___ ___ ___   ___ ___ ___
(1 2 3 4   5 6 7   8 9 10 11 12 13 14   15 16 17)

___ ___   ___ ___ ___ ___ ___ ___ ___ ___, ___ ___ as the Lord thy God commanded
(18 19   20 21 22 23 24 25 26 27 28 29)

thee" (Deuteronomy 5:12).

Shh, Be Still

Maze

Behold, mine house is a house of order.
—Doctrine and Covenants 132:8

• • • • • • • • • • • • • • • • •

Write the words that correspond with the clues below. Begin with the ★. Read the answers on the lines beginning with number one to learn the words to a song about a special place to go on the Sabbath day.

★our	we	a	be	humble	peace	dear	sing	sacred	patience
thoughts	is	our	smart	quietly	place	love	sweet	pure	and
calm	while	joy	thee	grateful	of	clean	kind	can	bless
chapel	will	to	we	Father	caring	pray	or	enter	good

1. ★___________
2. Down 3 spaces ________________
3. Right 1 space, up 2 spaces ____________
4. Up 1 space, right 1 space ____________
5. 6 spaces right __________________
6. Down 1 space, left 3 spaces ____________
7. Down 2 spaces, left 2 spaces ________________
8. 5 spaces right _____________
9. Up 2 spaces, 4 spaces left ______________
10. Up 1 space, 2 spaces right _____________
11. Down 3 spaces, 2 spaces left ______________
12. Up 1 space, 3 spaces left _________________
13. Up 2 spaces _________________
14. 6 spaces right _______________
15. 1 space down, 2 spaces right ________________
16. 2 spaces down, 3 spaces left _______________
17. 4 spaces left, 2 spaces up ______________
18. 2 spaces left _________________
19. 2 spaces down, 1 space right ________________
20. 3 spaces up, 2 spaces right ________________
21. 2 spaces down, 2 spaces right _____________
22. 2 spaces left ____________________

("Our Chapel Is a Sacred Place," *Children's Songbook*, 30)

A COVENANT PLACE

Hidden Message

That will I seek after; that I may dwell
in the house of the Lord
all the days of my life.
—Psalms 27:4

• • • • • • • • • • • • • • • • •

Draw a line from letter to letter in a zigzag pattern starting with the first letter on the top line, dropping to the second letter on the bottom line, and so forth. When you finish, repeat the pattern starting with the first letter on the bottom line and draw a line to the second letter on the top line. Place each letter on the line below to reveal a message about a special place.

I	M	O	O	E	N	O	T	E	E	T	E	E	O	E	E	P	A	E
I	L	G	V	I	T	G	S	H	E	R	H	S	T	M	M	D	L	Y

___ ___ ___ ___ ___ ___ ___ ___ ___ ___ ___ ___ ___ ___

___ ___ ___ ___ ___ ___.

___'___ ___ ___ ___ ___ ___ ___ ___ ___ ___ ___ ___ ___ ___ ___ ___ ___ ___.

(*Children's Songbook*, 95)

A Special Temple

Letter Clue

And the house which I build is great:
for great is our God above all gods.
—2 Chronicles 2:5

• • • • • • • • • • • • • • • • •

Find the word for each definition. Write the numbered letters below to complete the scripture about a special temple. Look up the scripture when you're through.

1. A covenant or oath ___ (26) ___ ___ (7) ___ (3) ___ (12) ___ ___ (30)
2. Very tired ___ ___ (5) ___ (24) ___ (33) ___ (4) ___ (29)
3. Your male parent ___ (8) ___ ___ (23) ___ ___ (2) ___ (32)
4. When you do what your parents ask you to do ___ (10) ___ ___ (28) ___ (17)
5. Intelligence and knowledge ___ (18) ___ ___ (13) ___ (11) ___ ___ (25)
6. The opposite of wrong ___ ___ (20) ___ (9) ___ (22) ___ (1)
7. A place to learn ___ ___ (21) ___ (19) ___ ___ (15) ___ (27)
8. The opposite of illness ___ (14) ___ (6) ___ (31) ___ ___ (16) ___

"For the ___ (1) ___ (2) ___ (3) ___ (4) ___ (5) ___ (6)   ___ (7) ___ (8)   ___ (9) ___ (10) ___ (11)
___ (12) ___ (13)   ___ (14) ___ (15) ___ (16) ___ (17),   ___ (18) ___ (19) ___ (20) ___ (21) ___ (22)
___ (23) ___ (24) ___ (25) ___ (26) ___ (27) ___ (28)   ___ (29) ___ (30)   ___ (31) ___ (32) ___ (33)"

(1 Corinthians 3:17).

FAMILIES ARE FOREVER

Scripture Find

• • • • • • • • • • • • • • • • •

Each scripture below has a missing word. Find the word, read the clue, and put the correct letter on the lines below to complete a thought about families.

1. "She openeth her mouth with wisdom; and in her tongue is the law of____________" (Proverbs 31:26).
   If the missing word is kindness, *write the letter* **O**. *If it is* truth, *write the letter* **C**.

2. "Children,________ your parents in all things: for this is well pleasing unto the Lord" (Colossians 3:20).
   If the missing word is follow, *write the letter* **H**. *If it is* obey, *write the letter* **R**.

3. "By this we know that we _______ the children of God, when we ______ God, and keep his commandments" (1 John 5:2).
   If the missing word is serve, *write the letter* **E**. *If it is* love, *write the letter* **D**.

4. "For I did liken all___________ unto us, that it might be for our profit and learning" (1 Nephi 19:23).
   If the missing word is truth, *write the letter* **M**. *If it is* scripture, *write the letter* **A**.

5. "And visit the house of each member, and exhort them to _______vocally and in secret and attend to all family duties" (Doctrine and Covenants 20:47).
   If the missing word is pray, *write the letter* **I**. *If it is* speak, *write the letter* **P**.

6. "Organize yourselves; prepare every needful thing; and establish a ________, even a ________ of . . . learning" (Doctrine and Covenants 88:119).
   If the missing word is church, *write the letter* **C**. *If it is* house, *write the letter* **N**.

7. "And all saints who remember to keep and do these sayings, walking in obedience to the ________, shall receive health in their navel and marrow to their bones" (Doctrine and Covenants 89:18).
   If the missing word is commandments, *write the letter* **E**. *If it is* Lord, *write the letter* **T**.

8. "Inasmuch as parents have children in Zion, . . . _____ them to understand the doctrine of repentance, faith in Christ the Son of the living God, and of baptism and the gift of the Holy Ghost by the laying on of the hands" (Doctrine and Covenants 68:25).
   If the missing word is teach, *write the letter* **D**. *If it is* help, *write the letter* **E**.

"The family is _____ _____ _____ _____ _____ _____ _____ _____ of God"
1 2 3 4 5 6 7 8

("The Family: A Proclamation to the World," paragraph 7).

Glorious Place

Matching

The Lord who shall suddenly come to
his temple.
—Doctrine and Covenants 133:2

Match the following clue phrase in the left column with the corresponding answer in the right column. Place the letter for the clue answer on the line with the corresponding number.

1. Ordinance performed for the people who have died	S. twelve
2. House of the Lord	F. white
3. I'm made of gold and sit up on top of the temple	O. temple
4. Age that you can begin to do temple work	H. baptisms for the dead
5. My water purifies and cleanses one from sin	D. reverence
6. Room in the temple where families are sealed	O. sealing room
7. The color of clothing worn in the temple	U. Angel Moroni
8. Special card required to enter the temple	E. baptismal font
9. When couples are sealed together in the temple	O. eternal marriage
10. A special feeling you have in the temple	G. temple recommend

___ ___ ___ ___ ___   ___ ___   ___ ___ ___
1 2 3 4 5   6 7   8 9 10

High on a Mountain Top

Crossword

Who shall ascend into the hill of the LORD?
or who shall stand in his holy place?
—Psalms 24:3

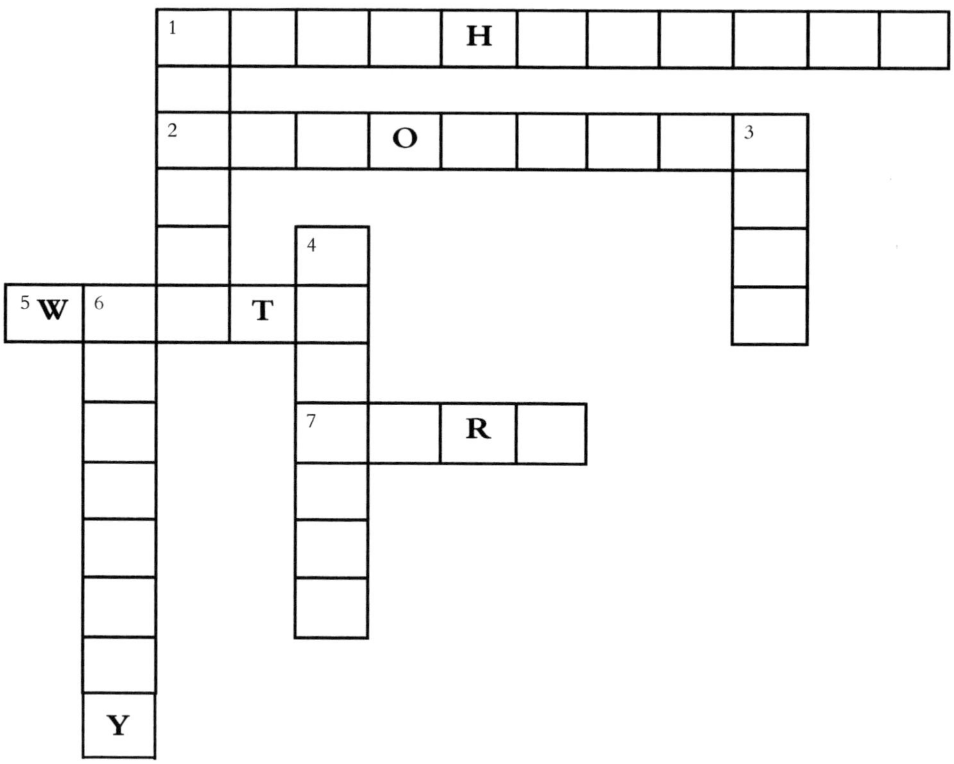

Across

1. The type of priesthood needed to perform ordinances in the temple
2. A special card needed to enter into the temple
5. The color of the clothing worn in the temple
7. The sign on the outside of each temple says, "Holiness unto the ________."

Down

1. The gold statue on the top of the temple
3. The ordinance performed in the temple when you turn twelve: Baptism for the ___.
4. The name of the ordinance that marries couples for eternity
6. The name of the prophet during the time that most of the temples have been built

After completing the crossword puzzle, unscramble the bold type letters to reveal what is required of us to enter into the temple: We must be _____________.

LATTER-DAY TEMPLE FIRSTS

Matching

Establish a house, even a house of
prayer.
—Doctrine and Covenants 88:119

• • • • • • • • • • • • • • • • •

Match each temple with a "first" fact about it (in parentheses is the year each was dedicated). Then put the underlined letter from the match on the blanks below (according to the matched number) to spell out a message found on every temple.

1. Kirkland	E. First temple built in Africa (1985)
2. St. George	S. First temple built in the 20th century (1919)
3. Cardston, Alberta	N. First temple built in South America (1978)
4. New Zealand	I. First temple built in southern hemisphere (1958)
5. Sau Paulo	L. First temple built outside the United States (1923)
6. Johannesburg	H. First temple built in the latter days (1836)
7. Swiss	O. First temple completed in Utah (1877)
8. Hawaii	S. First temple built on the European continent (1955)

"____ ____ ____ ____ ____ ____ ____ ____ to the Lord!" (Exodus 28:36).
1 2 3 4 5 6 7 8

On Every Continent

Logic

The Prophet Elijah was to plant in the hearts of the children the promises made to their fathers, Foreshadowing the great work to be done in the temples of the Lord in the dispensation of the fulness of times.
—Doctrine and Covenants 138:47–48

• •

Temples dot the earth and are on nearly every continent. One temple from each continent is in this puzzle. From the clues below, find which temple is on each continent and in which order they were dedicated (the numbers represent when each of these temples was dedicated with number one being the earliest dedication). Cross out the choices in the boxes according to the clues to reveal the answers.

1. The first and last temples dedicated are on continents that begin with the letter "A."
2. The temples on the continents of South and North America are the third and fifth temples dedicated (neither of them is the Preston temple).
3. The temples on the continents of Asia and North America were dedicated second and third, and the temple on the continent of Africa was not the last temple dedicated.
4. The Asuncion temple is on either the continent of Asia or South America, and the temple on the continent of Europe was dedicated fourth.
5. The Seoul and Johannesburg temples are not on either of the American continents (North or South).
6. Toronto was not on a continent that began with "A" or "E," and the Brisbane temple was the last one dedicated.
7. The Johannesburg and Preston temples are not on the continent of Asia. The temple on the continent of Europe begins with a letter after the letter "M."

	Continent						Temple					
1	Africa	Asia	Australia	Europe	North America	South America	Asuncion	Brisbane	Johannesburg	Preston	Seoul	Toronto
2	Africa	Asia	Australia	Europe	North America	South America	Asuncion	Brisbane	Johannesburg	Preston	Seoul	Toronto
3	Africa	Asia	Australia	Europe	North America	South America	Asuncion	Brisbane	Johannesburg	Preston	Seoul	Toronto
4	Africa	Asia	Australia	Europe	North America	South America	Asuncion	Brisbane	Johannesburg	Preston	Seoul	Toronto
5	Africa	Asia	Australia	Europe	North America	South America	Asuncion	Brisbane	Johannesburg	Preston	Seoul	Toronto
6	Africa	Asia	Australia	Europe	North America	South America	Asuncion	Brisbane	Johannesburg	Preston	Seoul	Toronto

Where We Can Turn for Peace?

Code

And verily I say unto you, let this house be built unto my name, that I may reveal mine ordinances therein unto my people.
—Doctrine and Covenants 123:40

Under each letter below, write the letter that comes before it in the alphabet. Continue through to the end and it will reveal a message of a peaceful place to go.

I P V T F   P G   U I F   M P S E

___ ___ ___ ___ ___   ___ ___   ___ ___ ___   ___ ___ ___ ___

Path to the Temple

EZ Maze

The great work to be done in the temples of the Lord in the dispensation of the fulness of times, for the redemption of the dead, and the sealing of the children to their parents.

—Doctrine and Covenants 138:48

Follow the path to the temple.

START

In His Temple

Missing Letter Words

But in the last days it shall come to pass, that the mountain of the house of the LORD shall be established in the top of the mountains, and it shall be exalted above the hills; and people shall flow unto it.

—Micah 4:1

Every other letter is missing from the phrases below. The letters are listed in alphabetical order in the box beside the phrase. Replace each letter to find phrases that tell about how the pioneers prepared for their journey. The scripture references have the answers if you get stuck.

1. H_ t_u_h_ d_i_y _n _h_ t_m_l_.
(Luke 19:47)
a a e e e e g i l p t t

2. l_t _s _o _p _o _h_ m_u_t_i_ o_ t_e _o_d.
(Isaiah 2:3)
a e e f g h l n n o r t t u u

3. _u_n _h_ h_a_t _f _h_ f_t_e_s _o _h_ c_i_d_e_.
(Malachi 4:6)
a e e e e h h l n o r r r r t t t t t

4. _p_a_ o_ h_s _l_r_.
(Psalms 29:9)
e f g i k o s y

5. _e_c_ a_d _r_a_h _e_u_ C_r_s_.
(Acts 5:42)
a c e h h i j n p s s t t

6. T_e _o_d _s _n _i_ h_l_ t_m_l_.
(Psalms 11:4)
e e h h i i l o p r s y

LDS Puzzle Pals

Answer Key

• • • • • • • • • • • • • • • • •

Baptism

Called of God to Baptize—page 1

John the Baptist
River Jordan

Clean and Pure—page 2

C	H	U	R	C	H	O	F	J	E	S	U	S	C	H	R	I	S	T	
	I							R	E	P	E	N	T	A	N	C	E		
	N	M																	C
	T		M	I	S	S	I	O	N	A	R	I	E	S					O
	E			E								S							M
	R				R						B	A	P	T	I	Z	E	D	M
	V		P			S	E				D	C						S	A
W	I		R				I			O		R					E		N
O	E		A				G	O	O			A				S			D
R	W		Y				H	H	N			M			S				M
T			E				T					E		E					E
H			R			S						N	N						N
Y					E	C	H	O	O	S	E	T	H	E	R	I	G	H	T
				I							I								S
			R							W	A	T	E	R	F				
		P	U	R	I	T	Y									A			
																	I		
J	O	H	N	T	H	E	B	A	P	T	I	S	T					T	
																			H
	G	I	F	T	O	F	T	H	E	H	O	L	Y	G	H	O	S	T	

Elements of Baptism—page 3

1. A broken heart and a contrite spirit
2. Baptized even by water
3. Baptism of fire and the Holy Ghost
4. Authority from Jesus Christ to baptize
5. Preach repentance and remission of sins

First Things First—page 4

1. Ordinances 2. Gospel
3. Faith 4. Repentance
5 Immersion 6. Holy Ghost
Articles of Faith 1:4

Follow Jesus Christ—page 5

1. Jesus Christ
2. Repentance
3. Disciples
4. Baptismal font
5. Eight years old
6. Holy Ghost
7. Book of Mormon
8. Mission

"Baptism by immersion for the remission of sins" (Articles of Faith 1:4).

Keep the Commandments—page 6

"I want my life to be as clean as earth right after rain.
I want to be the best I can and live with God again" (*Children's Songbook*, 103).

Prepare for Baptism—page 7

1. Immersion
2. Prayer
3. Confirmation
4. Ordinance
5. John the Baptist
6. Apologize
7. Truth
8. Bible
9. Priesthood

"You much repent and be baptized, in the name of Jesus Christ" (Doctrine and Covenants 18:41).

The Lord's Way—page 8

A. John B. the
C. Baptist D. Judea
E. Immersion F. Jordan

The Way We Are Baptized—page 10

1. Repentance 2. Follow
3. Holy Ghost 4. Witness
5. Commandments 6. Eight
7. Little 8. Authority
9. Jesus
Immersion

Choose the Right

Choose Your Words—page 11

Holy Ghost

Do As I'm Doing—page 12

"We believe in being honest, true, chaste, benevolent, virtuous, and in doing good to all men; indeed, we may say that we follow the admonition of Paul—We believe all things, we hope all things, we have endured many things, and hope to be able to endure all things. If there is anything virtuous, lovely, or of good report or praiseworthy, we seek after these things" (Articles of Faith 13:11).

Fruits of the Spirit—page 13

	T	I	U	R	F							E
									P		C	
F	A	I	T	H					E	N		S
S		G				E			A			S
P			O		V			R	C			E
I	J	O	Y	O			E		E			N
R			L		D	P						K
I					M	N						E
T				E			E					E
G	E	N	T	L	E	N	E	S	S			M
									S			
G	N	I	R	E	F	F	U	S	G	N	O	L

Leap of Faith—page 14

"I Will Follow God's Plan for Me"

Look to the Savior—page 15

"I would that ye should look to the great Mediator, and hearken unto his great commandments; and be faithful unto his words, and choose eternal life" (2 Nephi 2:28).

This Brings Me Joy—page 17

"Choose the right way, and be happy,
I must always choose the right" (*Children's Songbook*, 160–161).

Word of Wisdom Choices—page 18

Don—"Tobacco is not good for man."—video
David—"Hot drinks are not for the body."—song
Mary—"Health in the navel"—puzzle
Cathy—"Every herb and fruit"—game

Your Best Choice—page 19

1. Honesty
2. Prayers
3. Reverence
4. Right
5. Health
6. Book of Mormon
7. Family
8. Covenants
9. Thankful
10. Word of Wisdom

"Choose you this day whom ye will serve; but as for me and my house, we will serve the Lord" (Joshua 24:15).

Shine Your Light—page 20

"Therefore let your light so shine before this people that they may see your good works and glorify your Father who is in heaven" (3 Nephi 12:16).

FAITH

Amazing Faith—page 21

"We believe in God the Eternal Father and in His Son Jesus Christ and in the Holy Ghost" (Articles of Faith 1:1).

Believe in the Lord Jesus Christ—page 22

1. Christ
2. Sorry
3. Follow
4. Prayer
5. Baptism
6. Believe
7. Temple
8. Heavenly Father
9. Sunday

"Faith is knowing the Lord will hear my prayers each time I pray" (*Children's Songbook*, 215).

Faith Is . . . page 23

1. Grain of mustard seed
2. Thy faith hath saved thee.
3. Children of God
4. Obey and observe
5. Faith to be healed
6. Signs follow those that believe

First Principle—page 24

"We believe that the first principles and ordinances of the Gospel are: first, Faith in the Lord Jesus Christ" (Articles of Faith 1:4).

Have Faith—page 25

"And now as I said concerning faith—faith is not to have a perfect knowledge of things; therefore if ye have faith ye hope for things which are not seen, which are true" (Alma 32:21).

Perfect Faith—page 26

"And he commandeth all men that they must repent, and be baptized in his name, having perfect faith in the Holy One of Israel, or they cannot be saved in the kingdom of God" (2 Nephi 9:23).

Power from Above—page 27

Courageously

Quiet Friend—page 28

"Listen to the still small voice! Listen! Listen!
When you have to make a choice. He will guide you always."
(*Children's Songbook,* 107)

Words of Faith—page 29

Answer: Obedience

Across

1. Prayer
5. Walk (by)
8. Jesus Christ
9. Forgiven
10. Live (by)

Down

2. Ask
3. Doubt (not)
4. Increase
5. Word of God
6. Believing
7. Learning

FAMILY

A Mother's Work—page 31

"A person bright and lovely is my mother dear" (*Children's Songbook*, 203).

FHE Assignments—page 32

Benjamin—scripture
Cindy—treat
Jeannie—lesson
Michael—game
Thomas—prayer

Family Ties—page 33

Answer: eternal

Sister	Grandma
Father	Brother
Uncle	Mother
Grandpa	Aunt

Heaven on Earth—page 34

"Pray in your families unto the Father, always in my name, that your wives and your children may be blessed" (3 Nephi 18:21).

Our House—page 35

"Establish a house, even a house of prayer, a house of fasting, a house of faith, a house of learning, a house of glory, a house of order, a house of God" (Doctrine and Covenants 88:119).

Song in My Heart—page 36

1. I	5. A	8. F
2. H	6. D	9. E
3. B	7. J	10. C
4. G		

Together Forever—page 37

"Sacred ordinances and covenants . . . in holy temples make it possible . . . for families to be united eternally" ("The Family: A Proclamation to the World, paragraph 3).

Who Am I?—page 38

I am a child of God.

One Eternal Round—page 39

Across	Down
2. You	1. Mother
4. Grandma	3. Father
5. Brother	7. Aunt
6. Grandpa	
8. Uncle	Answer: Family
9. Sister	

Follow Jesus Christ

Are We Willing?—page 41

"And he said unto the children of men: Follow thou me. Wherefore, my beloved brethren, can we follow Jesus save we shall be willing to keep the commandments of the Father" (2 Nephi 31:10).

Covenant Challenge—page 42

A=5, B=10, C=15, D=20, E=25, F=30, H=35, I=40, L=45, M=50, N=55, O=60, R=65, S=70, T=75, U=80, V=85, W=90, Y=95

"And now because of the covenant which ye have made ye shall be called the children of Christ" (Mosiah 5:7).

His Only Begotten Son—page 43

"For God so loved the world, that he gave his only begotten Son, that whosoever believeth in him should . . . have everlasting life" (John 3:16).

Jesus Said—page 44

1. Obey the commandments (Deuteronomy 11:27)
2. Give heed to the prophets (D&C 1:14)
3. Learn of me (Doctrine and Covenants 19:23)
4. Search the scriptures (John 5:29)
5. Pray to the Father (Moroni 4:2)

O Lord, My Redeemer—page 45

See last page of answer key, page 110.

These Things We Do—page 46

"And we talk of Christ, we rejoice in Christ, we preach of Christ, we prophesy of Christ, and we write according to our prophecies, that our children may know to what source they may look for a remission of their sins" (2 Nephi 25:26).

Live Like His Son—page 47

Across	Down
3. Commandments	1. Obey
5. Listen	2. Scriptures
7. Prayer	4. Serve
8. Blessings	6. Faith
9. Heed	7. Prophet

Son of God—page 48

"For unto us a child is born, unto us a son is given: and the government shall be upon his shoulder: and his name shall be called Wonderful, Counsellor, The mighty God, The everlasting Father, The Prince of Peace" (Isaiah 9:6).

Let Him In—page 49

"Be thou humble; and the Lord thy God shall lead thee by the hand, and give thee answer to thy prayers" (Doctrine and Covenants 112:10).

MISSIONARY

Be a Missionary—page 51

O	B	E	D	I	E	N	T	P	
		A		E	L	D	E	R	S
A	G		P			D	A	E	C
U	O			T	L		C	A	R
T	S	P	I	R	I	T	H	C	I
H	P		O			Z		H	P
O	E	W			T		E		T
R	L			I	W	A	L	K	U
I			S	E	R	V	E		R
T	D	I	L	I	G	E	N	C	E
Y	V		F	A	M	I	L	Y	S
P	R	I	E	S	T	H	O	O	D

Be a Shepherd—page 52

Feed my sheep

Missionary Songs—page 53

Proclaim

Missionary Talk—page 54

"They shall speak as they are moved upon by the Holy Ghost" (Doctrine and Covenants 68:3).

Prepare to Be a Missionary—page 55

Ruth polished shoes.
Ellie studied the scriptures.
Tom ironed shirts.
James made dinner.

We Share Truth—page 56

"We are as the army of Helaman. We have been taught in our youth. And we will be the Lord's missionaries to bring the world His truth" (*Children's Songbook*, 172–173).

What Do We Teach?—page 57

Word of God

Heavenly Servants—page 59

1. Things
2. Wisdom
3. Learn
4. Fellow
5. Service

Preach the Word—60

Across

2. Walk
3. Testify
6. Prayer
8. Teach
9. Service

Down

1. Baptize
2. White
4. Scriptures
5. Spirit
7. Gospel

PIONEERS

Crossing the Plains—page 61

Answer: Family

1. Sickness
2. Mountains
3. Oxen
4. Campfire
5. Prairie
6. Walking
7. Wagon
8. Faith
9. Happy

Pioneer Handcarts—page 62

Valley

Wagon Gear—page 63

1. Medicine
2. Animals
3. Lantern
4. Kettles
5. Blankets
6. Tent
7. Bow and arrow
8. Tools
9. Seeds
10. Scriptures
11. Clothing
12. Washboard

Westward Trek—page 64

Emily	Kettle
Mandy	Clothing
Sarah	Lantern
Missy	Blanket
Lizzie	Food

Pioneers Today—page 65

"Walking our pathway with heaven in view" (*Children's Songbook*, 215).

Searching for Zion—page 66

W	G					O	X	E	N	G	
A	N	C	H						N		
L	I		A		P	L	A	I	N	S	
K	T		N	M			G			U	D
I	N		D		P	N				P	R
N	A		C		I	F				P	A
G	L		A	S		A	I			L	W
	P		R			M		R		I	T
F	A	I	T	H		I			E	E	S
						L				S	E
			P	R	A	Y	I	N	G		W
I	L	L	N	E	S	S					

O, Pioneers—page 68

1. Putting in spring crops
2. Covenant and promise
3. Teams, wagons, provisions, clothing
4. With a pure heart
5. Praise the Lord with singing
6. Ready to go to a land of peace
7. Prepare for those who are to tarry

Pioneer Journeys—page 69

Covenant

Prophets

Gospel Truth—page 70

The gospel restored to the earth. Joseph Smith Jr.

Hallowed Ground—page 71

Brigham Young
This is the place.

He Said It! He Did It!—page 72

Prophesies

Heavenly Father's Voice on Earth—page 73

"We thank thee O God for a prophet" (Hymn 19)

Old Testament Prophets Teach—page 74

"Surely the Lord God will do nothing, but he revealeth his secret unto his servants the prophets" (Amos 3:7).

Organized Like Times of Old—page 75

"We believe in the same organization that existed in the Primitive Church, namely, apostles, prophets, pastors, teachers, evangelists, and so forth" (Articles of Faith 1:6).

Power on Earth—page 76

"The priesthood is restored, the truth made known to man,
That God has spoken to the earth, his power is here again"
(*Children's Songbook*, 89).

Six Be's to Follow—page 77

1. Grateful
2. Smart
3. Clean
4. True
5. Prayerful
6. Humble

What a Prophet Does—page 78

1. Teach
2. Lead
3. Guide
4. Foretell
5. Reveal
6. Seer
7. Speak

Which Prophet Said That?—page 79

David O. McKay: "Every member a missionary."
Ezra Taft Benson: "Read the Book of Mormon."
Gordon B. Hinckley: "Come to the temple."
Spencer W. Kimball: "Lengthen your stride."

Sabbath Day

At Church—page 81

Worship

Blessed Be the Day—page 82

"And the inhabitants of Zion shall also observe the Sabbath day to keep it holy" (Doctrine and Covenants 68:29).

Day of Rest—page 83

"Remember the sabbath day, to keep it holy" (Exodus 20:8).

Modern Day Plates—page 84

2					M	O	R	M	O	N			I
N		J	A	R	O	M						N	
E								J	A	C	O	B	
P			1	N	E	P	H	1		R			
H	M								O		O		E
I	W	O	R	D	S	O	F	M	O	R	M	O	N
		A	S				I	H	P	E	N	3	O
		M		I	H	P	E	N	4		I		S
H	E	L	A	M	A	N							
		A				H			E	T	H	E	R

Sabbath Day Choices—page 85

"And on the seventh day God ended his work which he had made; and he rested on the seventh day from all his work which he had made" (Genesis 2:2).

Sabbath Day Gift—page 86

Sacrament

True Worship—page 88

Take upon you the name of Christ; and worship God, in whatsoever place ye may be in, in spirit and in truth" (Alma 34:38).

What Do You Do on the Sabbath?—page 89

1. Attend church
2. Read scriptures
3. Sit reverently
4. Fast and pray
5. Visit others
6. Family activities

When We Go to Church—page 90

1. Family
2. Sacrament
3. Chapel
4. Obedient
5. Prayer
6. Talk
7. Tithing
8. Bishop

"Keep the sabbath day to sanctify it, as the Lord thy God hath commanded thee" (Deuteronomy 5:12).

Shh, Be Still—page 91

"Our chapel is a sacred place; we enter quietly. Dear Father, while we sing and pray, our thoughts will be of thee"
(*Children's Songbook*, 30).

TEMPLES

A Covenant Place—page 92
"I love to see the temple. I'm going there someday" (*Children's Songbook*, 95).

A Special Temple—page 93
1. Promise
2. Sleepy
3. Father
4. Obey
5. Wisdom
6. Right
7. School
8. Health

"For the temple of God is holy, which temple ye are" (1 Corinthians 3:17).

Families Are Forever—page 94
Ordained

Glorious Place—page 95
House of God

High on a Mountain Top—page 96
Answer: We must be worthy.

Across	Down
1. Melchizedek	1. Moroni
2. Recommend	3. Dead
5. White	4. Sealing
6. Lord	6. Hinckley

Latter-day Temple Firsts—page 97
"Holiness to the Lord" (Exodus 28:36).

On Every Continent—page 98

Continent	Temple
1. Africa	Johannesburg (South Africa)
2. Asia	Seoul (Korea)
3. North America	Toronto (Canada)
4. Europe	Preston (England)
5. South America	Asuncion (Uruguay)
6. Australia	Brisbane (Australia)

Where We Can Turn For Peace—page 99
House of the Lord

In His Temple—page 101
1. He taught daily in the temple.
2. Let us go up to the mountain of the Lord.
3. Turn the heart of the fathers to the children.
4. Speak of his glory.
5. Teach and preach Jesus Christ.
6. The Lord is in his holy temple.

O Lord, My Redeemer—page 45

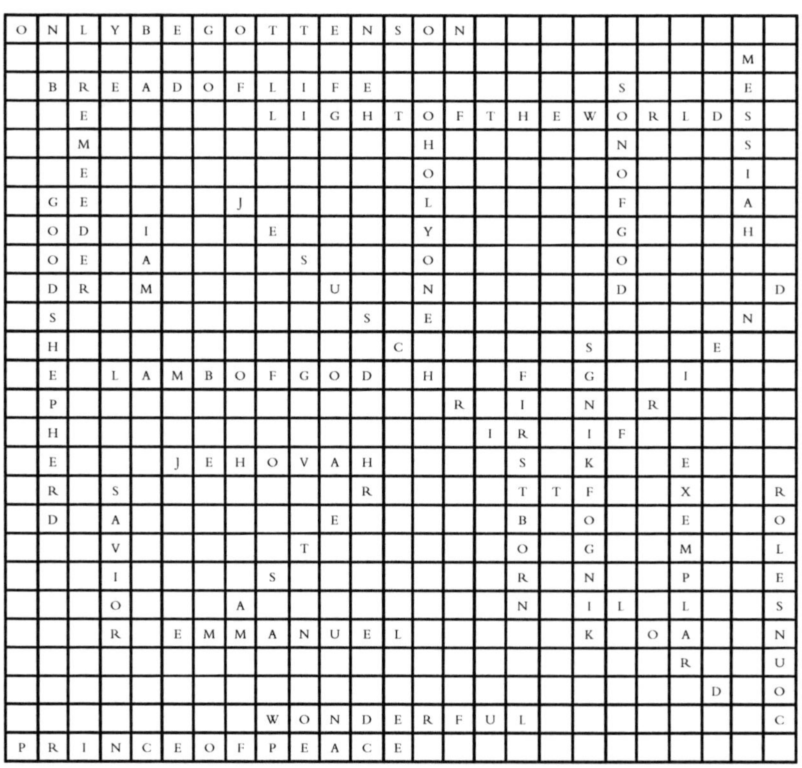

Doodle Pages

About the Authors

MaryAlice Wallis

MaryAlice Wallis, a Washingtonian most of her life, graduated from Western Washington University with a degree in speech pathology and audiology. She has served as Primary president, Young Women's president, and on the Stake Primary board. Writing has been a passion throughout her life, and she has published puzzles and activities in the *Friend* magazine. MaryAlice currently resides in Longview, Washington, with her husband, David, and their four home-educated children.

• • • • • • • • •

C. G. Lindstrom

C. G. Lindstrom grew up in the army until her father retired and the family moved to Utah. She graduated from Utah State University in Logan, Utah, with a degree in early childhood education and elementary education. She is a voracious reader and loves doing puzzles of all kinds. She has written puzzles and stories for the *Friend* magazine. Now she lives in Washington with her husband, Dan, and two almost grown sons. During the school year, she teaches kindergarten at a local elementary school. She has served in Primary and Young Women, and is currently the Relief Society president in her ward.

0 26575 79946 0